ENEMIES
of the STATE

ENEMIES
of the STATE

Tim Priest

NH
NEW
HOLLAND

To those wise old street cops of decades ago, who protected,
nurtured and encouraged me.
I hope I have done you proud.

To my wife Karen, without whom this book
would not have been possible.

To my father, Rusty Priest AM: A soldier's soldier
who has helped make sure Australia's war veterans
will never be forgotten.

To my children Karen, Hayley, Liam, Evin and Marlee for
their patience and understanding.
To my mother and my sister Carole-Anne.

In memory of Morgan Samuel Ogg, 1963-2004,
journalist, political advisor and great mate
and Micki Braithwaite.

First published in Australia in 2009 by
New Holland Publishers (Australia) Pty Ltd
Sydney • Auckland • London • Cape Town

1/66 Gibbes Street Chatswood NSW 2067 Australia
218 Lake Road Northcote Auckland New Zealand
86 Edgware Road London W2 2EA United Kingdom
80 McKenzie Street Cape Town 8001 South Africa

A record of this book is held at the National Library of Australia

ISBN 9781741108705

Publisher: Fiona Schultz
Publishing Manager: Lliane Clarke
Proofreader: Bronwyn Phillips
Designer: Hayley Norman
Production Manager: Olga Dementiev
Printer: McPhersons Printing Group
Cover photograph: Getty Images

10 9 8 7 6 5 4 3 2 1

CONTENTS

FOREWORD

Tim Priest came to his role as whistleblower reluctantly. A young police officer in the western Sydney suburb of Cabramatta in the 1990s, he faced a dilemma about lunch. If he left the police station and walked down the street to get a sandwich, he would feel duty-bound to arrest the flagrant drug dealers and petty criminals he passed along the way.

In the surreal world of NSW policing at the time, a police officer doing his duty was bound to antagonise his superiors. Priest and his colleagues were expected to turn a blind eye to crimes they saw occurring every day on their beat, for if police did not record crimes then officially they did not occur, and the crime statistics for Cabramatta looked rosy.

This was a time when Cabramatta was the heroin capital of Australia, when heroin dealers infested the streets, addicts from all over Sydney came to commit crimes to fuel their habit, when home invasions and murderous turf battles were a way of life. Residents said it was like living in a war zone. They barricaded themselves inside their apartments, and kept their children home from school. Drug dealers and criminals had free rein and residents were lucky to get out on day release.

Yet, under the mentality of the NSW Police Service, the official crime index declared Cabramatta to be one of the safest suburbs in Sydney.

It was the same all over NSW, as a police service brought to its knees by fruitless corruption inquiries suffered under an interventionist Labor government, more interested in spin than substance, and a hapless imported British commissioner who never understood the troops he led. Criminals became emboldened as they realised frontline police were increasingly powerless. It was what is called a reverse broken windows policy—the complete opposite of the zero tolerance police work which had so effectively cleaned up crime in New York.

Between 1993 and 2001, the crime rate in NSW soared, and Australia led the Western world in burglary and violence offences.

Out on the beat, Tim Priest was in despair. With four children of his own, he hated seeing another drug addict dead, hated the disillusion and fear on the faces of those he was supposed to protect. He hated not being able to do the job he had signed up for. He and a few fellow officers began to defy their superiors. And in 2001, called up to a NSW Parliamentary enquiry into policing, he told the truth. He testified that front-line police were being expected to turn a blind eye to drug-related crime.

The forces of the state mobilised to discredit him: his evidence was denied, his career destroyed, and he was derided by senior police and politicians as a 'disgruntled detective.'

It is a tribute to his courage and fortitude that he kept talking about what he knew, about the official pattern of denial about drugs and gang crime. His words have proved prophetic in the years since, which have seen the Macquarie Fields and Cronulla Riots, a bikie gang murder at Sydney airport in broad daylight, gun battles in suburban KFC carparks and Middle Eastern and bikie gang warfare which have overwhelmed the ability of authorities to contain them.

With his experience on the frontline in Sydney's toughest beats, from Kings Cross to Cabramatta, Priest, a decorated police veteran, knows where to look to unravel the bureaucratic and ideological roots of the crisis that grips policing today, and stops dedicated officers from doing their jobs.

This book is testament to his forensic abilities and to his courage.

Miranda Devine
Sydney, 2009

INTRODUCTION

I grew up in the 1960s, when the world was a different place. Many people of my era say it was a better, slower and safer world than what it is today. At that time, most Australian kids had a fairly good idea of what they intended to do for a career well before they left school. It is so different today, with most young people, from my own experience as a parent, leaving that choice till the very last minute, usually the day they receive their HSC results!

I also grew up in a stable and safe environment. I was the son of a distinguished professional soldier, Rusty Priest AM. My uncles and all of my dad's mates were returned servicemen from World War II.

I sat enthralled for hours as they spoke of their experiences in the war, of their adventures as young soldiers and the pride they felt in having defended their country. From my earliest memories, I wanted to be a soldier like my father, my uncles and my neighbours.

I also had a burning desire to be a policeman. I think this was first nurtured by a kindly old police sergeant who managed our local rugby league team when I was a youngster. He was a big, impressive man with a disarming sense of humour. Many of us 'young rebels' benefitted not only from his discipline, but from his kind words of advice and the odd crime story, often told to a hushed group of young boys who listened to his descriptions of fatal car crash scenes, murders, shootouts and brawls. It's funny looking back on those talks and wondering whether anything of that nature goes on in today's 'politically correct' society.

I am sure the old sarge caused more than one or two odd nightmares among the assembled group, but it made those kids respect the policeman not only for his entertainment value, but for giving us an insight into what policing was about. From those talks I decided I had a problem. I wanted to be a cop, but I also wanted to be a soldier.

So I asked the old sarge what he thought I should do. He told me that many of the policemen he worked with were soldiers before they had become cops and he said that they made the best policemen, because they had lived a bit more than the fresh-faced young police recruits he often saw.

I followed his advice and 11 days after my seventeenth birthday, along with 40 other young Australians, marched into Kapooka, near Wagga Wagga in country New South Wales, the home of the Australian Army's 1st Recruit Training Battalion, 1RTB.

During my nine years in the army I don't think I ever stopped learning about life, about human dynamics and, importantly, about a sense of duty and a sense of honour, something I believe every young man needs to help guide them through life—never more so than now.

The army not only physically toughens up its soldiers, it also toughens them up mentally for what might lie ahead. That is what the old sarge had in mind when he gave me that advice all those years ago. I enjoyed every minute of my time in the army, but the desire to be a NSW policeman had never left me, so I applied and was accepted.

I joined the New South Wales Police Force during the final three months of my army career in 1982. I had saved up all my leave and went to the famous old Redfern Police Academy while I was still technically a serving soldier. I was discharged from the army six days before being sworn in as a constable in the New South Wales Police Force. Neither the army nor the Police Department were aware of this slight anomaly and I still wonder how I would have explained this 'unusual' situation had I been asked.

On graduating from the Academy I was stationed at No. 22 Division, Liverpool, which took in the infamous Green Valley Housing Estate nearby, known amongst the cops as 'Dodge City' for its violence and high rates of serious crime.

I was in 'the job' for just a few days when I attended my first fatal traffic accident at Moorebank, involving a stolen car. The car had been wrapped around a telegraph pole and the occupants were killed instantly. It was a horrific scene, with the smell of blood and the mangled bodies visible through the wreckage. It was customary for the supervising sergeant to ask after the welfare of a newly minted constable at their first 'deadun', as deceased persons were known. But the 1st Class Sergeant just remarked, 'He's an ex soldier, this won't worry him.' In a way he was right, although there are few policemen who can honestly say that the years of seeing mangled bodies, tending to innocent victims of crime and violence and dealing with the relatives of those victims in their worst hours, does not take a toll on their physical and mental health. This may not be apparent immediately, but gradually over time, the defence mechanisms fail and the cop begins to remember many of his worst jobs.

One of the reasons I, and most young police, survived our first 12 months was due solely to the guidance we were given by several sergeants and inspectors. Many of these men had over 25 years of policing experience, some with nearly 40 years in the job. There was little in the world that these men did not know or had not experienced first-hand in their careers. Not only did they nurture their young cops, they protected them from danger where possible and encouraged them to go on to bigger and better things.

These legendary old school cops were disappearing when I first joined, but I have enduring memories of these now forgotten policeman—such as Sergeant 1st Class Peter McMurray, Sergeant 1st Class Jimmy Morgan, Sergeant 1st Class Don Risso, Sergeant 2nd Class Mel Clews, Sergeant 2nd Class Alf Gregory, Sergeant 2nd Class Glen Denholm—the list is endless. They are all now just memories. Today's young cops no longer have these great old cops as mentors, protectors and advisers and the Police Force is a lesser body without them.

Despite being sent straight from the academy to such a tough and unforgiving place as Liverpool, I was indeed fortunate. I learned more about policing in those first 12 months than many of my fellow constables did at quieter stations.

At Liverpool, barely a week would pass without a serious MVA (motor vehicle accident) and some would be indeed double or triple fatal MVAs. Then there were the brawls, the armed robberies, the murders, the suicides, the violent domestics— every shift at No 22 Division was interesting and nearly always adrenalin-charged.

Indeed when I joined my classmates for my secondary training after 12 months, you could see the changes in the 'pros' (probationary constables) who had been working at the big, busy stations in Sydney's western suburbs, stations like Liverpool, Blacktown, Fairfield, Mt Druitt, Penrith, and Bankstown. These young cops had aged just a little more than the others and were quieter and a little more reserved. I would realize many years later just why that was. It was probably the first signs of stress that had come with the traumatic scenes they had dealt with in their first 12 months.

Within less than two years I was involved in my first police shooting. It was the Queen's Birthday long weekend in June in 1984 and a suburban shootout left one person dead, a police sergeant critically wounded and two other civilians who were lucky to survive that most unpredictable of police incidents— the violent domestic. For a policeman involved in their first shooting, nothing is ever the same again.

I worked hard as a 'pro' and was rewarded with a short stint with the Liverpool Drug and Vice Unit where I worked with three of the best detectives I had ever seen—Ray King, 'Bluey' Ducker and Peter Harris. From that short experience, I became hooked on plain clothes or detective work, and after just 18 months in uniform I was given a position upstairs in the detectives' office as a trainee detective. It was the start of a three-year apprenticeship, culminating in the detective's course and being granted the highly prestigious designation of

Detective. Barely a year into my plain clothes career, I was transferred to the Drug Squad at the Criminal Investigation Branch (CIB) of the NSW Police.

I was very fortunate to have gained entry into the CIB at such a junior rank and to see some of the great detectives of that era in action. At the Drug Squad, I grew my hair ridiculously long, grew a beard and wore some of the loudest and brightest shirts seen on Sydney's streets in decades. Cruising the city in an unmarked V8 Holden Commodore executing search warrants on drug dealers' premises, doing surveillance on major drug dealers and gathering intelligence from underworld figures made this the greatest job on earth. No one ever wanted to take holidays, the job was that good.

There was also the downside, such as the near fatal shooting of fellow Drug Squad Detective Michael Drury, a good mate still to this day.

A brief stint in the Kings Cross Drug Unit during Operation Explorer taught me about the seedy underbelly of Sydney and how dangerous a place it can be for the unsuspecting and the uneducated. If Sydney had an outdoor sewer, then in the 1980s Kings Cross was it. I could never quite get my head around the way that the squalor and the hopelessness of some parts of the Cross sat just a few streets away from the most expensive real estate in Australia. They were two different worlds separated by just a few hundred metres.

In 1987, I was seconded to the newly formed National Crime Authority (NCA) under the former Supreme Court Judge Justice Donald Stewart, who was himself a former New South Wales policeman.

At the NCA I worked with some of the best detectives in

the country, including Australian Federal Police Commissioner Mick Keelty, Australian Crime Commission head and former NSW Homicide Squad detective Alistair 'Jock' Milroy, Mark Plumb, a highly regarded Northern Territory detective and many others.

The current Shadow Attorney General in NSW, Greg Smith, was a senior lawyer working at the NCA, along with Tim Sage, an Assistant Commissioner of the Police Integrity Commission.

I worked mainly on the Italian Organised Crime Reference, code named Romeo, which looked into current and historical crimes involving the 'honoured society' that is the mafia. Many of the names that have cropped up on the Channel 9 hit television series *Underbelly* were known to the NCA back in the mid 1980s—names such as Trimboli, Sergi, Grassby and many many more. I was also privileged to meet and speak to Barbara Mackay, the widow of Griffith's anti-drug crusader, Donald Mackay. I remember Barbara Mackay as a courageous and remarkable woman.

One of the final jobs I did before leaving the NCA involved the arrest and charging of five men, including a Guatemalan diplomat at the Regent Hotel in Sydney, over the importation of 88 pounds (40 kilograms) of high grade heroin through Sydney Airport. All of the offenders received very lengthy sentences and that seizure remained for a time one of the biggest in Australia's history.

Having expended vast quantities of adrenaline in the 1980s, and with a young family, I moved to a suburban detective's role, firstly at Liverpool and then the infamous Green Valley. Later I worked at one of the most challenging police stations any cop can work at—Redfern. Both Kings Cross and Cabramatta can shock you, but Redfern leaves you with a lasting impression that includes a sense of guilt, that we as a society have failed miserably when it comes to our First Australians. It is a national disgrace and despite the rhetoric, the marches and the apologies, they don't seem to be a whole lot better off than previous generations. Someone has to do something to save this remarkable indigenous society before it is too late.

In 1997 I was promoted to sergeant and stationed at the now infamous Cabramatta Police Station. Cabramatta was another world, a world so far removed from the average Sydneysider that seeing really was believing.

The level of violence was something few police in this country have ever, or will ever, experience. The levels of drug dealing, organised crime, including extortion and money laundering, were breathtaking. The extent of human misery and the disregard for human life by some sections of the community was indescribable. It left Kings Cross for dead, literally.

I began to do my bit for global warming by catching the train to and from work and I think I lasted about two weeks. If I wasn't stopping the addicts from getting on the train at Cabramatta with me, then I was helping a few off at the various stations along the way home. On one memorable occasion, I was meant to start the shift at 7am. I got off the train at Cabramatta in plenty of time to walk the short distance to the police station but along the way there was a deceased drug addict lying on the steps of the local library. He had died overnight and had been there for many hours in view of passing pedestrians who no doubt thought it was just another overdosed heroin addict— such was the attitude to drugs, druggies and life within that community.

Cabramatta was certainly the heroin capital of Australia.

It was also the homicide capital. The shootings, stabbings, machete attacks, murders and attempted murders and malicious woundings along with the many fatal heroin overdoses made Cabramatta an out and out crime capital.

In the late 1990s, as the police were fighting a losing battle against the tide of drugs and crime, they were also fighting an enemy within. For all its policing problems, the one shining light was the total absence of police corruption, which is a lasting tribute to the honest hardworking cops that served in the suburb. However, police management changed in 1996 under the Carr government with the appointment of Police Commissioner Peter Ryan. The fallout from the Wood Royal Commission into the NSW Police Service in 1997 hung over police officers across the state and cast a pall of suspicion about their integrity that still lingers to this day.

Under Ryan's new policing theories and statistics, Cabramatta apparently became 'safer than Roseville' on Sydney's affluent north shore. This claim by Ryan in February 2000, widely reported in the press, marked the beginning of his slide from power. Morgan Ogg, then a Channel 7 reporter, ran a spoof on the 6 o'clock news of visiting the 'new' Sydney crime hot spot, Roseville, complete with film coverage of an elderly gentleman dressed in tweed, wearing a matching tweed hat and walking a small poodle around a leafy park and then panning the camera back to Cabramatta, the safer of the two suburbs, and showing speeding police cars, ambulances, crime scenes, bodies covered by blankets, visual images of bullet riddled shops and restaurants. It was brilliant and tragic—tragic in the sense that political and police media spin had reached a level where the reality on the ground had been lost.

November 1999 marked the beginning of an all-out drugs and gang war in Cabramatta with more than 40 shootings, resulting in a number of murders and attempted murders playing out across Australia's television channels as the full horror of the Cabramatta story began to emerge. There had in fact been a report warning of this situation compiled by the NSW Police Asian Crime Unit, predicting the scale and type of violence that came to pass. That report, known as the Cook Report, was to become a highly controversial subject in the ensuing fallout over Cabramatta.

Cabramatta at that time mirrored the overall state of health of the NSW Police Service. It was in a perilous state, with little hope of recovery unless drastic steps were taken to restore a balance between good policing and media policing that had appeared with the appointment of the Police Commissioner Peter Ryan. Somebody had to say something about the damage that was being inflicted not only on the Police Service but on the community in general. That, eventually, was me. I could not let an institution that I had adored since childhood, an institution that had given up the lives of over 230 police officers in the line of duty, to become so demoralized and inept that it was no longer a force, but a farce.

A year later in 2000 a specially set up NSW Parliamentary Inquiry, the Cabramatta Policing Inquiry, began hearing evidence of the massive failure by police in Cabramatta to control drugs and crime.

In 2001, along with four other Cabramatta policeman— Greg Byrne, Bob Francis, Vince Fusca and Chris Laird—I gave evidence of the failings of police tactics in the suburb. My evidence was to become the most controversial. I accused senior police of failing to heed the signs of a gang war that was developing in Cabramatta in 1999 and spilled over into 2000, of abandoning the suburb and its migrant citizens. The media storm that followed was unbelievable and the fallout was equally so.

I also alluded to the wider problems confronting the NSW Police after the Wood Royal Commission. That was to be my biggest 'offence'. Criticising the Wood Royal Commission was akin to denying the holocaust. I soon came under the scrutiny of a group of journalists and academics who had campaigned for the Wood Royal Commission along with their political contacts.

By the time The Cabramatta Inquiry, under Asian-born Australian Helen Sham-Ho, completed its hearings it would become one of the most widely reported and successful Parliamentary inquiries in the state's history. It brought about real change. It gave the suburb back to its citizens and ousted the gangsters and drug dealers that had turned it into a living nightmare.

The fallout from that inquiry was equally sensational. The Police Minister, Paul Whelan, a wealthy hotelier, along with the Education Minister John Aquilina, were sacked. Police Commissioner Peter Ryan resigned and the careers of a number of senior police were halted.

My career predictably came to an end in 2002, a year after I gave evidence before the inquiry—the NSW Police is an unforgiving organization and there were a few inside the Police Service that believed I had crossed the line by speaking out against senior ranking police and as such my 'papers had been stamped'. My career would probably have ended sooner, but for the support and encouragement of people such as Alan Jones, Miranda Devine, Piers Akerman, Ray Hadley, Ray Martin and Steve Barrett, from the media, as well as the political support of the NSW Opposition including John Brogden and Kerry Chikarovski and of course the Police Minister that replaced Paul Whelan, the enigmatic Michael Costa. At great political risk he had me transferred into his Ministry to get me out of the firing line in the wake of the Cabramatta Inquiry. Michael is a remarkable man who was ahead of his time, and was sincere and ethical.

In 2003, along with my friend and mentor, American-born anthropologist Dr Richard Basham, I co-authored the best-selling book *To Protect and To Serve*. Little has changed since then, except that now, more than ever, we need a police force experienced in the old ways, to combat the rising menace of Middle Eastern crime, outlaw motorcycle gangs (OMCGs) and a general breakdown in public order on our streets, where the drunk and drug affected are again making some areas of Sydney no-go zones, although the authorities will no doubt dispute that title.

In the ensuing years, journalists loyal to Peter Ryan and the Wood Royal Commission have waged a battle to discredit those who challenged them and their ideas on law and order. Some of these so-called investigative journalists either failed to uncover, or worse failed to report on, the cover-ups, some criminal, some beyond belief, that occurred directly within the very body charged with investigating police corruption in NSW, the Wood Royal Commission. Why? Because to do so, would attack the very institution they revered and because those in command ultimately became too close to some of these journalists.

The only people that were held accountable for corruption were members of the NSW Police Force. In many instances this was well founded; in many other instances, it was flawed and maybe even contrived. The 'old guard' police officers who had been trained at the Redfern Police Academy were seen as a major problem in the new police service under Peter Ryan. There were many attempts to get them out so that a new breed of 'academic' cops, that according to Ryan could investigate a traffic accident in the morning and conduct a murder enquiry in the afternoon, could take their rightful place. This was mad hatter policing at its very best. That type of policing, the British model, is said by many critics to be largely to blame for crime statistics in Britain, especially in some areas of London where violent crime appears out of control.

There was also a subtle strategy by the Carr government to gain political control of the police force and do something no other government in NSW in almost 140 years had been able to do—control it. Simple as that. The NSW Police had resisted political control successfully for generations and that had irritated and frustrated many politicians. Neville Wran, the former NSW Premier, once remarked governments could not rule in NSW without the support of the Police. Bob Carr, courtesy of the Wood Royal Commission fallout, managed to control the NSW Police and it has remained an arm of the NSW Government ever since.

Hunting down the 'old guard', as Chris Masters of the ABC *Four Corners* program once described old style cops, by the Wood Royal Commission was done so in the finest traditions of the Grand Inquisitors of the thirteenth century. Many innocent police officers lost their careers on the say-so of a cast of characters that included paedophiles, bent cops, drug dealers, thieves and liars but who were all given the special status of 'Royal Commission witness', and therefore their evidence was taken over that of the experienced policemen.

For decades, successive NSW Governments relied on the Police Force to keep its citizens safe. Tough, uncompromising police ruled gangs and drug dealers with an iron fist. Sure there were controversies, there was corruption and there was more than a hint that change was needed. But what the Wood Royal Commision did was to dismantle that Police Force and attempt, but fail, to rebuild a new one, with the assistance of lawyers, academics, so-called investigative journalists and a few recycled 'old school' cops reborn as academics. It was a disaster looking for a location. That location has turned out to be the NSW Police Force.

Unable to predict and prevent levels of organised crime few thought possible in this country 20 years ago, the NSW Police Force now lurches from one disaster to the next. The Cronulla riots, Redfern riots and Macquarie Fields riots are just a few of the notable public order debacles. This is in addition to the emergence of Middle Eastern crime gangs, outlaw motorcycle gangs, Pacific Islander crime, the apparently endless blowing up of ATMs across the city and a type of lawlessness on the streets few could have imagined.

Those that could have stopped this madness are long gone. Those that remained in the 1990s were hunted down by the Wood Royal Commission. The old school cops that once brought safety and security to the community streets for over a century became, on a single vote in Parliament in 1994, *enemies of the state*.

1.

FOR THE GOOD OF THE COMMUNITY: THE WOOD ROYAL COMMISSION

When the Inquisitor arrived he would invite all people who wished to confess themselves guilty...to come forward. Suspect(s) were given a 'time of grace' to denounce themselves. If they did so they were obliged to name and furnish detailed information about all other heretics known to them.

The Inquisitor was ultimately interested in quantity. He was quite prepared to be lenient with one transgressor, even if he were guilty, provided he could cull a dozen or more others, even if they were innocent.

The Inquisition, Baigent/Leigh, 1999.

On 11 May 1994 at 7.58pm, Mrs Deirdre Grusovin, a Labor Opposition Member in the New South Wales Parliament, rose before Parliament and commenced the final debate on the need for a Royal Commission into corruption allegations against members of the New South Wales Police Service. By the time John Hatton, the Independent Member for the NSW parliamentary seat of the South Coast and one of the driving forces behind the debate into police corruption in New South Wales, rose to address his fellow Members, the public gallery had filled and included senior New South Wales Police Officers.

New South Wales was about to experience an unprecedented inquiry into the nation's oldest, largest and most controversial constabulary, the New South Wales Police. Hatton began by saying:

> We have to believe in the institution [the NSW Police], as the Premier said—and many honest police want to sincerely believe, some of them do, in the institution. A Royal Commission will lance the carbuncle and the rottenness will come out.

The resulting Wood Royal Commission would be anything but the minor surgery involved in lancing a boil. It would inflict wounds on the police service that would be beyond any post-operative treatment and the institution would be forever changed. The Wood Royal Commission would cut the heart and soul out of the once flawed but revered NSW Police.

John Hatton, a former school teacher, had been campaigning against entrenched police corruption for over 16 years. He had named former and serving NSW police officers under parliamentary privilege for being corrupt and had endured personal insults from parliamentarians with close police contacts.

In the debate in May 1994, Hatton used former Police Superintendent Brendan John (Jack) Whelan as an example of a corrupt policeman that he wanted exposed and removed. Whelan had been the Chief Investigator on the Woodward Royal Commission into Drug Trafficking (1977-1980) which centered on the murder of Donald Mackay in Griffith in 1977.

Hatton argued for the need for 'independent' investigators not belonging to, or connected with, the NSW Police, to be involved in the Wood Royal Commission into Police Corruption.

When the debate finished, the Members of Parliament broke for the vote to be taken as to whether or not a Royal Commission was warranted. There were 46 for the amendments and 45 against. By one vote, NSW not only had a Royal Commission into Police Corruption, but one that employed only outside investigators. There were no NSW police officers attached to the Royal Commission.

Little did Hatton or the other parliamentarians realise the implications that decision would have years later when the actions of some Royal Commission investigators would be called into question in a most serious way. Little did Hatton realise also that the Commission would never investigate his original points, but instead had a different agenda.

The Member for Cabramatta at that time, John Newman, also spoke on the debate and expressed his views on the growing crime problems in the western Sydney suburb of Cabramatta. It would be one of the last occasions that John Newman would attend the New South Wales Parliament. Just four months later, on 5 September 1994, he was gunned down at his home by local Cabramatta gangsters on the orders of an aspiring Labor Party politician, Phuong Canh Ngo. The murder stunned the country as the first political assassination in Australia's history. Hours earlier on that same day, Phuong had been at a café in Sussex Street Haymarket, not far from the NSW Labor Party headquarters, with a few senior elected and non elected ALP officials. At a time when Parliament was focussing on police corruption, it is ironic that a politically inspired assassination was taking place in Cabramatta.

Like many police officers, I viewed the announcement of a Royal Commission into Police Corruption with some reservation. I knew I didn't have anything to fear, but I had seen the fallout of a similar commission, The Fitzgerald Inquiry into Possible Illegal Activities and Associated Police Misconduct, led by Tony Fitzgerald QC, which had been held in Queensland in 1987.

I had mates that were serving Queensland police officers then and they had, more than once, described the pain and humiliation of a police force placed under the microscope and the years it took to repair the damage to their reputation in the eyes of the public. The public relied on a 'balanced media' coverage of the day's news but often received only the most sensational coverage of evidence, with a focus on sordid details of individual corrupt police officers. These corrupt individuals made up a small percentage of the total force, but the public mindset was understandably shaped into thinking the majority must be corrupt.

Commissions of Inquiry are given the mandate to explore and expose. As such they are forums for many allegations, which they are entrusted to seek the truth about. It is usually the role of Counsel Assisting to co-ordinate all facets of the commission, including the gathering, examination and subsequent presentation of evidence.

Counsel Assisting also coordinates adversely mentioned witnesses and those called 'rollover' witnesses, often in a highly charged environment. 'Rollover witnesses' are often crucial. They consist of the people who are prepared to 'name and shame' other people from within their own organization that they suspect of wrongdoing. Rollover is a common police phrase for someone who is prepared to give information on the basis that they will not be prosecuted themselves.

The integrity of a Royal Commission and its public image is also a factor in their operation. I believe that this public image was so important to the Wood Royal Commission that it often ignored the potential damage to individual police officers because it feared the damage to the Commission itself that would be incurred if the public were to find out that unsupported testimonies given inside the hearings were either wrong, or were invented by witnesses. In other examples, poor intelligence gathering on the part of Wood Royal Commission investigators also caused significant damage to individual police officers who were plainly innocent of the allegations made against them.

When NSW Premier John Fahey announced the details of the Wood Royal Commission (1994-1997), which included His Honour, Justice James Wood QC as the Royal Commissioner and Gary Crooke QC, as Counsel Assisting, it appeared to be a formidable combination.

Gary Crooke had previously worked on the Fitzgerald Inquiry

and seemed a logical appointment.

The Royal Commission cast included a senior Australian Federal Police Officer, Nigel Hadgkiss, who was appointed as Director of Investigations (now Executive Director of the NSW Department of Public Prosecutions (DPP)). Senior Counsel included:

- James Black QC (now a NSW District Court judge).
- John Agius SC (was also Counsel Assisting the Royal Commission into the Australian Wheat Board in 2006 and the Royal Commission into the Western Australian Police in 2003).
- Virginia Bell (now a Judge of The High Court), and
- Patricia Bergin (now a NSW Supreme Court Judge).

The recruitment of interstate police to fill the investigator positions was carried out with 'positive vetting', according to Wood himself in an address in 1999. That positive vetting did not include a Royal Commission investigator from the Queensland Police, Paul Stevens, who was adversely mentioned in the Fitzgerald Inquiry for obtaining free drinks and meals at a premises known as 'Fantasy Photographs'.

Gary Crooke, who was Counsel Assisting the Fitzgerald Inquiry at the time Stevens was adversely mentioned, should have known the history of Paul Stevens.

Paul Stevens and a controversial former South Australian police officer, David McGinlay, would attract serious allegations of impropriety in a subsequent District Court matter involving the 'Kareela cat burglar'. Also known as the 'Toorak Cat', the criminal involved was codenamed YM1 by the Wood Royal Commission as he, like another informant KX15, would be granted special status as a Commission witness and his past, like that of KX15, would be conveniently forgotten (see The Kareela Cat Burglar chapter in this book).

With the staff recruitment completed and the premises set up, the Royal Commission investigators went to work. Their most prized recruit amongst rollover corrupt NSW police officers was Detective Sergeant Trevor Haken.

Haken admitted to gross corruption to the Royal Commission in closed court. Some people would refer to Haken as a whistleblower. Others described him as a corrupt policeman who saw an opportunity to save his own skin.

What is not widely known or acknowledged is that Trevor Haken was not the prize catch of the Royal Commission through their efforts alone. Haken had already been identified by NSW Police Internal Affairs to the Royal Commission and had been collecting information from him and acting on it. Many commentators say that he would have been charged anyway, despite the Royal Commission.

There is no doubt Haken's 'rolling over' was a watershed in terms of breaking the 'blue wall of silence' or cracking 'the brotherhood'. Soon other police involved in corrupt conduct would follow suit to the Wood Commission. There was some satisfaction amongst ordinary cops that those who didn't deserve to wear the uniform were being exposed and sent on their way. But there was also a good deal of resentment when good cops were named and shamed on the say so of bent cops, sometimes just to settle old scores.

What was not anticipated was the unprecedented media exposure that the Wood Royal Commission would generate relentlessly for nearly three years.

The only time the media took a break from revealing the

findings and consequences of the Wood Royal Commission was out of respect for Senior Constables Addison and Spears, who were gunned down in the New South Wales mid-north coast town of Crescent Head after attending a domestic dispute. Their names are now etched on the Police Wall of Remembrance along with some 230 New South Wales Police who have died on duty, a heavy toll by any standards for a police force operating in a supposed civilised society.

Media coverage of the Commission was relentless. If you picked up the morning newspapers, such as the *Daily Telegraph* or the *Sydney Morning Herald*, you were greeted with the day before's explosive testimony of corrupt cops or witnesses. If you switched on the radio, you got more of the same and then when your wife or kids switched on the television for the nightly news, it was even worse.

Day after day, month after month, for nearly three years, the New South Wales Police Force became a despised institution and those that worked for it were viewed with great suspicion by members of the public.

Defence lawyers seized on the moment and frequently mentioned aspects of the Wood Royal Commission while cross-examining police officers in completely unrelated cases about police interviewing techniques, no doubt to try and influence the jury as to the integrity and credibility of the police officer giving evidence. It did not matter that the individual police officer had never and would never be mentioned at the Royal Commission. The old crude saying that 'shit sticks to a wet blanket' was apt in the circumstances. The New South Wales Police Force became the largest wet blanket on the planet.

Indeed, such was the fallout and the resulting damage to the

New South Wales Police through this period, that many other states shied away from having similar inquiries into their own police forces purely because of the damage they saw inflicted on the nation's largest police department.

A considerable amount of material gathered by the Wood Royal Commission found its way to journalists. Exclusive stories were published containing biased statements against police officers who were subject to investigation by the Commission. No better examples of this are the Kareela Cat Burglar segment and the Task Force Bax segment (see chapters in this book). Material in a range of articles on those two subjects attracted unreasonable and biased media attention.

I will never forget one particular article in a Sydney Sunday newspaper during the Wood Royal Commission. The journalist said they had a key informant within the Wood Royal Commission and he had been 'told' that as many as 2,000 New South Wales detectives were suspected of being corrupt. It was not supported by any legitimate evidence given before the Royal Commission. It was absolutely demoralising for the many honest detectives that were still trying to do their jobs under the shadow of the Royal Commission.

Many police officers, including myself, believe that the Wood Royal Commission used an aggressive media strategy which involved providing information to journalists known to Royal Commission staff. That tactic helped make the Wood Royal Commission the most sensational inquiry in Australia's history. Whether that tactic was ethical is still being debated.

In fact, the Wood Royal Commission paid tribute to the media in its final report with this reflection:

The media coverage of the public hearings was extremely important in the early days in flushing out potential witnesses, in encouraging confidence in the work of the Royal Commission and in informing the public of the problems which existed. The mainstream coverage was largely accurate and responsive to suppression orders (such infringements as did occur being unintentional, acknowledged, and readily redressed) and the Commissioners are grateful for the care and professionalism that the regular reporters brought to the task.

Without a balanced and informed coverage of the Royal Commission, it is beyond question that the flow of information and of informants, which occurred would not by any measure have been achieved.

The Blackburn Royal Commission in the 1980s heavily criticised the NSW Police Service at the time for the treatment of a suspect in front of the media. The Blackburn Royal Commission made scathing criticism of the NSW Police in parading former superintendent Harry Blackburn before a staged media gathering when he was arrested, yet the Wood Royal Commission appeared to do the exact same thing through their aggressive media strategy, but on a larger scale.

The numbers and extent of corrupt police was overinflated, to such an extent that the Commission suspected that corrupt police would plant bombs in the Commission rooms and exposed this to the media, with television footage showing Army bomb dogs searching and sniffing out 'potential threats'. It was a farce that also contributed to a perception amongst the public that the NSW Police was not only corrupt, but dangerously so as well.

The Wood Royal Commission, I believe, became a cleverly managed 'theatre' that overemphasised the level and extent of corruption and justified its need to continue, well beyond its use-by-date.

There is no doubt that police corruption was in existence. However, that corruption was already being dealt with and the levels were diminishing year by year. What the Commission did was to sensationalise it to justify their own existence.

What is widely ignored is that this culture had already been changing, albeit slowly, under Commissioner John Avery, a deeply religious man and the first non-detective Police Commissioner in a generation. Avery had begun the painful task of changing the New South Wales Police. He disbanded the old Criminal Investigation Branch (CIB) and regionalised the Detective Squads into North, North West, South, and South West regions, with an Assistant Commissioner attached to each region. While this broke up existing power bases around the Criminal Investigation Branch, it led to other equally serious issues.

Was the Commission successful in tackling corruption? Yes, in some ways. It changed a police culture almost overnight but unfortunately the good officers went out with the bad. Police procedure was changed and the fundamental principles of policing were altered dramatically—we are now seeing the disastrous results of those changes. A great deal changed in the way police in NSW went about their work mostly, I believe, for the wrong reasons.

Ironically those changes have come back to haunt the New South Wales Police Force, not in terms of corruption, but in terms of organised crime. It is no accident that drug supply, drug distribution networks and their associated crimes continue to evolve in a size and nature not thought possible in this country.

Police corruption did not help the cause and, it has to be said, facilitated some of that growth, but not all of it. There was, according to former Assistant Police Commissioner Geoff Schuberg, a legendary corruption fighter in the New South Wales Police Force, 'nothing wrong with the CIB, just its supervision'.

Despite numerous remarks from politicians, journalists and radio DJs about the old squads, they were very effective in combating specialised crimes, such as drugs, motor vehicle theft and conversion, armed robberies and safe breakings, many of which appear to be out of control today. Many argue that the ATM robberies that are afflicting New South Wales at present and continue to defy all attempts to stop them, either by arrest or detection are a result of the changed structure and the lack of specialisation. It is now spreading interstate.

Rather than change the supervision and culture of the specialist squads, it was decided to eliminate them altogether. To some degree, the specialisation aspect of the Criminal Investigation Branch has re-invented itself in the form of strike forces, which are formed when specific serious or persistent crimes are occurring. There is any number of strike forces now operating in NSW because of serious and persistent crime. No senior police officer or politician will admit that the rebirth of specialist police crime squads is reflected in the strike forces now operating widely in New South Wales.

The problem with strike forces, however, is that they are

mostly temporary bodies and they are disbanded when the case is solved or becomes cold and the detectives working on those strike forces often do not have enough time to develop the specialised skills needed for some of the more unusual investigations these strike forces are set up for.

The need for specialised intelligence units is no more apparent than with the recent outbreak of outlaw motorcycle gang violence now sweeping across Sydney and the emerging threat of Middle Eastern criminals infiltrating the bikie gangs and bringing with them increased and unprecedented violence.

During and after the Wood Royal Commission, I couldn't help but think that somehow Justice Wood and his staff believed that a near perfect world existed outside the hearing rooms and that there were no justifiable reasons for corruption. In the sense of taking bribes, engaging in drug supply, fixing court matters and the like, there can be and never was a justifiable excuse. It is plain criminality.

But Wood continually refers to process corruption, or 'noble cause corruption', which he argued could never be excused. Noble cause corruption is often referred to as being done 'for the good of the community'. That is, where an offender is known or highly suspected of committing an offence, the police 'load him up' or plant or fabricate evidence to strengthen the case against him. A good deal of the Wood Commission Report mentions this behaviour and Wood makes no secret that he detests this practise, a practise stated in his final report that, 'commonly becomes linked with extortion, theft and other forms of corruption'.

You be the judge of whether the following example is serious corruption as outlined by his Honour in the final report:

Unofficial or unauthorised practises, such as putting suspected street drug dealers onto a train and banning them from an area.

That is just good old fashioned policing, but it is the type of policing that Wood found objectionable. What were police to do when confronted with rampant street dealing? Give the dealers numbers and allocate an area for them to operate in with equal opportunity?

Justice in New South Wales as I see it has never been about an even playing field, it is about the adversarial system of courts. It is about police continually playing catch-up with ever decreasing powers under the law and being further eroded through stated cases or Superior Court decisions.

Take, for example, judgments handed down by the Appeal Court and the High Court that have a retrospective impact on similar cases yet to go before the courts. It may be that police have acted in good faith for years when carrying out their jobs but suddenly, because of a High Court decision, that good faith may be deemed to be either illegal or wrong at law.

The often quoted Williams case in the 1980s had a dramatic impact on police procedure when arresting suspects.

In simple terms, according to the law in New South Wales, which is similar in most other states, police, when arresting a suspect, have to take that suspect to the nearest justice to be dealt with. It did not apparently allow police to interview that person in regard to his arrest between the time he was arrested and charged and placed before a court. The practise of detaining suspects for interview had been going on for decades with little opposition from the courts, but with the occasional complaint from the Bar.

When the Williams case was handed down in 1985 it threw many briefs of evidence into disarray (*R vs Williams*, 1985). Ultimately it fell upon individual Judges and Magistrates to decide whether evidence from the police would be allowed or excluded, and whether the practise of detaining suspects for interview was sufficiently bad enough for evidence of confessions to be excluded from the hearing.

Later, the NSW Parliament passed a law that allowed police to detain suspects in custody (with certain provisions) for a period of four hours that could be reviewed by a Magistrate and extended again. The old practise of police detaining suspects for interview eventually became law, but not before police briefs of evidence collapsed and opportunistic defence lawyers descended on courts screaming 'Williams, your Honour'.

Another legal decision involving wording on police search warrants saw matters dismissed with costs in many courts through no fault of the individual police officers concerned. It was simply the Superior Courts finding an illegality in the way search warrants were worded and deeming that those warrants were defective.

In most cases, search warrants are critical to how police uncover evidence of criminality. You can imagine the frustration and disappointment of police officers who have pursued habitual and dangerous criminals and have done everything by the rules and then months or even years later, the rules are changed and the goal posts shifted, and they are nearly always shifted in favour of the defendant.

The Wood Commission's final report was viewed by many as a

blueprint for massive reform in which a new Police Department would be born. The police would play strictly and utterly by the rules and true justice would be returned to New South Wales. But it was one-sided, or at least appeared to be.

As a result, we now have the police force that the Wood Royal Commission bequeathed to the citizens of the State of New South Wales. I am not alone when I view the New South Wales Police as almost 'impotent', too frightened to take on organised crime lest there might be corruption allegations again. It appears that the New South Wales Police Media Unit has become the single most important unit in modern day crime fighting methods employed by the NSW Police.

I have emphasised the Wood Royal Commission for two important reasons. The Kings Cross drug supply fiasco of 1996 and the Kareela cat burglar case show the hypocrisy of the 'do what I say, not what I do' attitude within some parts of the Wood Royal Commission.

The criticisms by Justice Wood highlight the immense gulf between the reality of life on the streets and the rarefied air inside the courts, which appear at times to be oblivious to the difficulties police officers on the street face in trying to protect the decent members of society.

What you will read next will shock you as those roles are reversed. The inquisitor, the Wood Royal Commission, suddenly realises that playing by the rules is not always convenient when trying to crack organised crime.

The behaviour and actions of Wood Commission staff in the examples I cover in this book show a differential attitude by the courts to this behaviour when it was brought, somewhat scarcely, to their attention in subsequent criminal trials.

I think the old adage, all men are born equal, just some are more equal than others' sums it up perfectly. Police officers have always been and will always be soft targets for all sorts of activists, particularly those that think the police are to blame for most of society's injustices.

2.

TASK FORCE BAX

In June 1996, the Wood Royal Commission was in the midst of a sensational segment about Kings Cross, led by one of the Counsel assisting the Royal Commission, John Agius SC. This segment saw a daily expose of corrupt Kings Cross police officers and became the new soap opera for those Sydneysiders who were following the Commission's hearings in the media. The chief witness, Trevor Haken, related stories of corruption and criminality in the police force. The community and the police service was sickened, and rightly so.

As these revelations of corruption were being aired on the nightly news channels, a very controversial law enforcement strategy was executed in extraordinarily secretive circumstances. I have absolutely no doubt that had this strategy been initiated by New South Wales Police and discovered during the Royal Commission, the police officers involved would have certainly received a front row seat at the Royal Commission, prime viewing on evening news reports, front pages of the daily papers and almost certainly a substantial prison sentence after a very public trial. But it remained secretive.

I begin with the Drug Misuse and Trafficking Act 1985, which states that:

> *A person who supplies, or knowingly takes part in the supply of, a prohibited drug is guilty of an offence.*
>
> *Defining 'supply':*
>
> *'Supply' includes to sell and distribute, and also includes 'agreeing to supply, or offering to supply, or keeping or having in possession for supply, or sending, forwarding, delivering or receiving for supply, or authorising, directing, suffering, permitting or attempting any of those acts or things.'*
>
> *Trafficking is 'the supply of drugs on more than one occasion'.*

A High Court judgment in 1995, known as the *Ridgeways* judgment, brought in a new level of accountability for police and altered the way police operations were conducted.

The High Court decision basically held that law enforcement officers (police and others) who induce or participate in criminal activities, even for the 'noble purpose' of apprehending major drug traffickers, were not immune from the criminal law and were likely to be found guilty of criminal offences themselves.

This judgment became well known in both legal and police circles and was widely reported. Interestingly, it used the 'noble purpose' explanation as a deterrent to potential police operations that may have crossed the line from legal to illegal.

In layman's terms, it meant that the end does not justify the means and was an issue emphasised at great length in the Wood Commission's final report on previous NSW police practises.

For decades, Kings Cross, in Sydney's eastern suburbs, had been infamous as a centre for sex, crime, drugs and corruption and there had been attempts, some serious, some not so serious, to rid the area of its reputation as Sydney's sin city.

However, the place just never got any better.

I worked at Kings Cross during 'Operation Explorer' in 1985 while attached to the Drug Squad and its replacement the Drug Law Enforcement Bureau (DLEB). To describe the area as seedy is being kind. Desperate people committing desperate acts to satisfy their drug habits occurred almost every minute. The area and some of it's business operators had little regard for the misery they caused to a great many people in both the drugs trade and the sex industry.

After a month or so at the Cross even hardened coppers became harder. You just couldn't allow yourself to feel much sympathy for the many miserable people that you came across, you just had to do your job as best you could. During Operation Explorer we did just that. Mass arrests were made over an extended period of some months. There was a noticeable reduction in the overt drug trade, but with the area set amongst mass apartment-style buildings, policing every square inch of Kings Cross/Darlinghurst was impossible. How do you constantly police the hallways of 20 and 30 storey apartment blocks?

What Operation Explorer did show was that vastly increased numbers of plain clothes police did in fact limit the impact of drug supply on the streets. However, like all operations of this nature, it required significant police numbers and significant resources to continue the assault on the drug trade. More importantly, it required the political commitment of the government of the day to keep such costly operations going for extended periods of time.

Just as the police began to get on top of the problem and limit the visible drug dealing on the streets, thereby decreasing the amount of crime associated with drug dealing, the plain clothes operation began to wind down and the Drug Squad detectives were pulled out to concentrate on major drug trafficking operations around the state. Kings Cross, with just a small drug unit, went back to trying to keep the dam from bursting open. Within a few years greater numbers of addicts flocked back to Kings Cross and demand increased supply.

Even so, it is interesting to point out that the drug dealing in and around Kings Cross could never rival that of Cabramatta, in Sydney's south west, Australia's heroin capital. However, Kings Cross still had major drug and crime problems that would only increase over time.

As with Cabramatta, all that was needed at the Cross was a commitment by both police and the government of the day to get their act together and bring about real change, not just rely on a few catchy media headlines to give the appearance of change.

There is no doubt that the honest police on the ground in Kings Cross did as much as they could with limited resources to attack the drug trade and arrest the dealers but with organised crime having such a vice-like grip on the area it was beyond the means of the Kings Cross Police to make any real progress in the war on drugs.

The Wood Royal Commission exposed corruption within

the Kings Cross Police Patrol, but there has been considerable debate as to whether this corruption involved protecting drug dealers and turning a blind eye to the heroin trade as much as the Wood Royal Commission and the media reported.

Had there been the commitment by senior police and politicians alike to clean up the mess, it is likely that Haken and other corrupt cops would have been swept up in the cleanout and either been sacked or forced to resign as a result of being uncovered.

While the Wood Royal Commission continued its investigations, the New South Wales Crime Commission stepped in to try and halt the volume of drug traffic running through the Cross.

A secret New South Wales Police Task Force was formed to investigate and prosecute organised crime and drug trafficking in Kings Cross. 'Task Force Bax' came into existence in March 1996 and was set up after an approach from the new Kings Cross Patrol Commander, Superintendent Mal Brammer, to the NSW Police Commissioner for help with tackling organised crime and drug dealing within his patrol.

Task Force Bax included some 32 detectives, many of whom had considerable criminal investigative experience. The Task Force was handpicked by senior NSW Police and was led by veteran Detective Superintendent Geoff Wegg and included highly regarded detectives such as Ray Lambie, Dave Rope and Paul Tuxford.

Within a short time of securing covert premises, members of Bax went to work and began building a vast database on drug dealers and other crooks frequenting the area. One of the initial targeted premises was a well-known drug haunt, the

Cosmopolitan Cafe, also known as Cosmo's.

It was in these premises that a mid-level street drug dealer would become involved in an unprecedented law enforcement operation that still to this day defies logic. That dealer, Gary Said, would later be given the codename of KX15 by the Wood Royal Commission (see chapter 1). For the purposes of this chapter, we will refer to him by his Wood Royal Commission codename, KX15.

Around the middle of 1996, Bax introduced undercover police into Cosmo's to make connections with heroin dealers operating from within the cafe. KX15 quickly came to the attention of Bax as a heroin dealer and was duly targeted for surveillance. Bax, using both electronic eavesdropping and physical surveillance, compiled considerable intelligence on the premises and the people that frequented it.

KX15 was a drug dealer of some notoriety around Kings Cross. He dealt heroin (smack) and cocaine (coke) in considerable quantities on a daily basis. He was a vital link in the supply chain from wholesalers such as the Bayeh brothers Bill and Louis and Peter and Roula Kay, to the street addict. Without his expertise and his connections, both sides of the supply line could not have operated as effectively as they did.

KX15's operation was a vast and profitable one. You can only guess as to the quantity of drugs supplied over a long period of time and the massive amount of money made. Indeed the Court of Criminal Appeal in November 2000 had trouble working out just how much drugs had been supplied in an appeal by Bill Bayeh against his sentence in the District Court in 1998.

The undercover police had little difficulty in scoring heroin from KX15 and over a period of time they were able buy heroin freely from him. These buys were strictly controlled within the Task Force and the drugs and money used for the buys were booked up as evidence for the proposed future prosecution of KX15.

Bax officers began formalising charges against KX15 for supplying an indictable quantity of heroin, which carried a lengthy prison term for him if convicted. According to Task Force Bax members, the evidence was both substantial and compelling.

As part of the New South Wales Crime Commission Eden reference, under which Task Force Bax operated, strict protocols required that Task Force Bax Commander, Superintendent Geoff Wegg, regularly informed the Wood Royal Commission of the activities of Bax.

Wegg attended the Wood Royal Commission in June that year and advised the Commission's Senior Counsel, Gary Crooke QC, that the Task Force was now in a position, through the evidence they had gained from Cosmo's Cafe, to arrest and charge a major mid-level heroin dealer, Gary Said, aka KX15.

However, it is from this meeting that the Wood Royal Commission appears to have gone from a Commission of Inquiry to that of a Commission policeman. What occurred next raises serious questions about the Wood Royal Commission's subsequent handling of KX15.

On that day in June 1996, when Superintendent Wegg attended the premises of the Wood Royal Commission and spoke with members of the Commission, he was told in no uncertain terms that Task Force Bax was not to arrest KX15, and were not to approach him on the streets of Kings Cross.

There can be little doubt that from the moment Superintendent

Wegg told the Wood Royal Commission about KX15 that the Commission knew what KX15's real value was to them. He would become an asset, as they would call him, in their quest for evidence of police corruption.

KX15 was already on the ground in Kings Cross, ready to be rolled over and rolled straight back onto the streets to become their eyes and ears on alleged police involvement in the Kings Cross drug trade. That was the plan at least.

KX15 was seen as a coup for the Royal Commission, which had been unsuccessful in obtaining witnesses to examine, and were facing the same difficulties that state police face every working day—trying to find a way into the darkened cavern that is organised crime.

Courtesy of Task Force Bax, they now had a witness looking for some serious assistance to help him with a major drug trafficking charge hanging over his head.

The Wood Royal Commission took over the management of KX15 and made sure they had total control over their new star witness by instructing Bax members to cease all surveillance and investigations on him.

The Task Force members were furious, but held their tongues and cooperated. However, within days of handing over the drug dealer KX15 to the Wood Royal Commission, Bax members noticed that he was still operating with impunity around Cosmo's Cafe and the nearby streets of Kings Cross.

Bax members watched as KX15 continued his drug dealing, day in day out, and grew angrier each day until they could contain their anger no more.

Task Force Bax detectives complained to Senior New South Wales Police through the appropriate channels. They brought the illegality to the attention of a number of their Commanders as well as the NSW Crime Commission. However, it appears that their complaints fell on deaf ears.

Within days, Royal Commission investigators, led by Investigator Detective Kieran Miller, an Australian Federal Policeman on secondment to the Royal Commission, raided the home of KX15. During the raid, KX15 was videotaped and tape-recorded talking to Royal Commission officers.

It is unclear whether drugs were found during the execution of the warrant but a considerable amount of cash was found at the premises. With KX15's drug dealing activities requiring him to work long hours, it is difficult to even think that he was gainfully employed away from the drug trade, making the cash highly suspicious and most likely, illegal.

During the raid, Detective Kieran Miller began to talk to KX15 about a task the Commission had in mind for him that would still allow him to carry on with his usual occupation as a drug dealer. KX15 was invited to become a Royal Commission informant, but with a difference. He could continue to sell drugs as he had done for some time, but he would have to be wired up and wear a tape so that not only would his drug bosses be implicated in this operation, but he would also expose any corrupt cops that were part of the operation.

Miller remained with KX15 while Counsel Assisting the Commission, John Agius, sought approval for what was about to become one of the most controversial law enforcement operations seen in this country.

John Agius visited the then Solicitor General of New South Wales, and subsequent President of the New South Wales Court of Appeal, the highly distinguished jurist, Keith Mason

QC. It appears, from subsequent court transcripts, that Agius, at the home of the Solicitor General on a Saturday afternoon, obtained verbal approval for the bold plan of allowing KX15 to continue supplying vast amounts of heroin and cocaine while being monitored by the Wood Royal Commission.

John Agius, in a later District Court hearing, testified that he had received 'oral advice' endorsing the proposed operation. This oral legal advice returned a drug dealer to the streets of Kings Cross along with his tainted money to continue peddling drugs to young Australians. Like many other ex-cops, I still cannot believe it.

To better explain why I am questioning the type of police operation the Royal Commission had initiated, let's go back just a year or two prior to this operation when state drug squads frequently used undercover police in what was known as buy/bust operations. That is, an undercover operative (UC) would be introduced to an informant who had access to larger suppliers within the underworld. Over a period of time, the UC would build a level of trust with the supplier and eventually negotiate the buying of larger quantities drugs from the supplier using police funds.

Often the UC was required to purchase larger amounts of drugs up front to prove that he was in the drug business and not a police agent. Those drug buys were always strictly controlled and both the money and drugs would be accounted for and booked up as exhibits for a future prosecution. Indeed, Task Force Bax, when using an undercover cop to snare KX15, videotaped all evidence of drugs they purchased from KX15 so that the buys would form legitimate and vital evidence in forthcoming prosecutions.

When the time came for the final buy/bust operation, a large-scale police operation would be commenced including the application for listening device warrants from a Supreme Court Judge. Together with appropriate security of the UC, surveillance would be placed on the targeted supplier many hours prior to the operation commencing. Often large sums of money would be withdrawn from police funds to show the supplier that it was indeed a legitimate sale and not a rip-off. Once the UC sighted the drugs, the axe would come down on the supplier and his associates who would be arrested and charged.

The only illegality that probably occurred was the buying of sample drugs to enhance the reputation of the UC in front of the supplier. But again, these sample buys were always booked up as an exhibit and were always used as evidence in Court.

Never did I see or hear of detectives condoning or engaging with criminal informants to supply drugs virtually unhindered in order to wrap a brief around a crook.

It would not only have been highly illegal, but foolish in the extreme. Had the Police Internal Affairs Branch become aware of such a practise, the axe would also have fallen on the detectives involved. It was unthinkable.

Not only would the police have been compromised in the ongoing supply of a prohibited drug, but what if, as quite often happens, an addict overdoses and dies? This would have been from a drug supplied by an agent for the police and as night follows day, manslaughter charges would surely have been considered if not preferred against any police involved.

The buy/bust operations had been going on for decades with the occasional murmur from defence counsels and the bench about 'agent provocateur' behaviour on the part of the police. That is, influencing a person to commit an offence that they may not have considered being involved in, but for the undercover police operative. This argument was usually overcome with the knowledge that first timers or amateurs don't usually, if ever, have access to the large quantities of drugs seized by police in these situations. Only high-level crooks usually have access to these quantities of drugs thereby making nonsense of police influencing them to commit crimes.

In 1995 that all changed by virtue of *Ridgeways* case, which introduced new restraints on the way police conducted buy/ bust operations and other stings. It caused considerable angst amongst police trying to infiltrate major drug trafficking syndicates and was yet another example of police constantly trying to play catch up with an ever-changing legal landscape.

In many instances, *Ridgeway* stopped police in their tracks when contemplating buy/bust operations. But how was it that under the auspices of the Wood Royal Commission an operation took place that was clearly outside the parameters set by the decision in *Ridgeway?*

Consequently, the evidence obtained from this operation was questioned in the trials of major drug dealers and was only permitted into evidence because the trial judge exercised a discretion to allow it, notwithstanding him finding that 'the course of conduct followed in relation to KX15 being sent back onto the street to engage in drug dealing' was, in the view of one District Court Judge, either illegal or improper.

What guidelines did the Wood Royal Commission operate under when crossing into the role of police operator as they did in the case of KX15?

Any operation they conducted should have been totally transparent. They should have been operating under the same guidelines I experienced in the mid-1980s as an investigator seconded to the newly formed National Crime Authority (NCA) under former New South Wales Policeman and Supreme Court Judge, Justice Donald Stewart.

The NCA was comprised of a number of 'references' or targets. Each of those references had senior counsel and lawyers, along with investigators and support personal, such as intelligence analysts, accountants and so forth.

The gathering of evidence was guided by advice taken from the NCA's lawyers and under the supervision of the Director of Investigations. I distinctly remember the many morning management meetings at the NCA, often with His Honour, Justice Donald Stewart in attendance. Various legal issues that may have affected the NCA's operations were always the subject of vigorous discussions between police and lawyers to satisfy the legal requirements of running covert operations.

All of the operations at the NCA were extremely sensitive and the targets that were being worked on, and who would ultimately be arrested, were very likely to defend the charges vigorously at trial. Everything had to be done correctly—no short cuts, no bending the rules. We understood the nature of the newly formed NCA and we wanted it to work.

The NCA was a quasi Royal Commission with extraordinary powers vested in it by the Federal and State Governments. To protect those powers and the reputation of the NCA there were extremely strict management guidelines that stretched from the top right down to the bottom rung. There was little deviance away from the game plan set by the NCA's executive and the executive was acutely aware of what each reference was doing and how they were doing it.

The NCA introduced me to a level of accountability and responsibility I had not seen before in my police career. If listening device warrants or telephone intercepts were to be initiated on a target, it would have to go through a strict protocol within the NCA before applications were made. Surveillance operations and investigations were similarly supervised at the top.

As mentioned, in many ways the NCA was similar in structure to the Wood Royal Commission. I can only assume that they too had management meetings each day and discussed important topics. The topic of KX15 must have been discussed at the highest levels of the Commission because of the controversial methodology being employed.

I cannot believe for one moment that John Agius or Kieran Miller acted alone in commencing such a controversial operation. In a letter cited by the highly respected former Homicide and Breaking Squad Detective, Mick McGann, in his submission, 'Who Guards the Guards', Gary Crooke QC confirms the Royal Commission model:

> The commission adopted a multi disciplinary team model for the conduct of its investigations. Each team comprised six investigators, two criminal analysts, two financial analysts, three solicitors and research and support staff. Teams were led by one of the Counsel Assisting the Commission, who consulted with me (Crooke).

Judging by the contents of that letter, it would appear that John Agius would have consulted with Gary Crooke QC, the Counsel Assisting the Wood Royal Commission. The final question remains as to whether His Honour Justice James Wood was also consulted.

In the transcripts of the judgment on Peter Kay, Bill Bayeh and Dominic Pedavoli on 17 August 1998, before New South Wales District Court Judge Justice Gibson, His Honour makes mention of the following:

> ...*it was a view that had been discussed with other more senior members of the commission...*

Who were the senior members involved?

The *Ridgeways* case was less than 12 months old when the Wood Royal Commission became involved with KX15.

Meanwhile, back in Kings Cross, to show that this unprecedented operation had the approval and knowledge at a high level within the Wood Royal Commission, the Counsel Assisting the Inquiry into the Kings Cross segment, John Agius SC, attended KX15's home and spoke with him. This conversation was recorded.

I have viewed some of the transcript material of the initial conversation between Kieran Miller and KX15 at his home during the search warrant and the subsequent approaches of both Miller and Agius in regard to KX15 becoming a Royal Commission agent. It makes interesting reading:

> *Kieran Miller: This is John Agius.*
> *John Agius: How are you, Sir? You know what the Royal*

Commission has been set up to do, to inquire into police corruption.

KX15: Why are you emphasising so much with me?

John Agius: Well, you're just one of many people we're looking at. But you've had dealings with corrupt police, you've said that yourself. We know you've been selling drugs which are sourced to Bill Bayeh and Peter Kay and we have evidence you've paid police.

KX15: What!...Paid Police? Hang on, hang on. I haven't paid Police.

In one sentence, KX15 denies and challenges the Wood Royal Commission's primary reason for recruiting him—to trap supposedly corrupt police.

This was a pivotal point in this investigation. This admission and the indignation shown by KX15 at the suggestion he was paying police should have questioned his value in this highly controversial investigation. The criminal behaviour of KX15 and his associates should have been referred back to Task Force Bax, which the Commission knew had already taken out a summons for his arrest. According to the tape recorded admissions of KX15 in front of John Agius and Kieran Miller, that's what it appeared to be, drug trafficking, not police corruption. That made it, I believe, outside the terms of reference the Parliament had set for this Royal Commission.

It is apparent that in the accusation that KX15 was supplying drugs and sourcing those drugs from Bill Bayeh and Peter Kay, the Commission were using evidence collected by Task Force Bax.

Does it follow that John Agius went to the Solicitor General with evidence gathered by Task Force Bax which concerned the supply of heroin and cocaine, but without any other cogent evidence that corrupt police were involved in protecting dealers such as KX15? Did John Agius have other reliable sources upon which to base his corrupt cops allegation? KX15 certainly wasn't a reliable source of information and he told John Agius so in no uncertain terms.

Undeterred by KX15's rebuff about corrupt cops not being involved in his operation, John Agius went on:

> *John Agius: I'm prepared to interview you on the basis that anything you say in the course of the interview or any document or thing that you produce will not be used against you in evidence in any criminal proceedings. All you have to do is to say that you'll do it.*
> *KX15: I understand that.*
> *John Agius: And all that will follow to you is benefit. Nothing that you do will be used against you in any way.*

What exactly this benefit entailed was to become a focus of evidence during a subsequent trial before the New South Wales District Court.

John Agius continued:

> *You know you're in a very serious position.*
> *KX15: Dangerous or serious?*
> *John Agius: Serious. What you've got to do now is just for a moment stop being a smartarse and make a decision about the rest of your life.*
> *KX15: You want me to go and make some money so I can rollover to you so I can piss off.*

From these taped conversations between John Agius and KX15, what appeared to be on offer was indemnity from offences he committed whilst participating in the Wood Royal Commission operation.

But somehow it seemed that KX15 believed he had a free pass not just from his sanctioned drug dealing with the Wood Royal Commission, but perhaps all criminal offences that he had committed.

Although KX15 was not formally being offered an indemnity from prosecution by the Wood Royal Commission, he assumed he was. He was going to 'piss off' after the job was done. KX15 subsequently was adamant that he had been shown or had 'seen' a document for his 'immunity'. However Judge Vinney eventually dismissed this in the District Court on 9 December 1999 despite there being an advice from a solicitor from the DPP seeking an undertaking for KX15 that found it's way (accidentally) into KX15's possession.

A few years later, KX15 was convicted of offences that had been investigated by Task Force Bax and when sentenced was given a 'letter of comfort' where the court was provided information about what he had done to assist the Wood Royal Commission in its operation. KX15 was sentenced to 400 hours of community service for his drug offences. Did he ever fulfill this Court ordered punishment?

When Kieran Miller was negotiating with KX15 at the Cross he set out the terms of the invitation:

> We['re] going to um...it's been decided to allow you to go back to the Cross area. We ('re) going to give you your money back that we took off you this morning. We are going to...and

we are going to let you continue what you would normally
do in the normal situation. So you would deal drugs under
a normal situation...You are not to go overboard with your
dealing, but you are to deal normally as you would normally
do and obviously you are to inform us on what you are doing
and who you are dealing with...As I said to you, you will be
dealing as you normally deal—no more or no less.'

And so began the short career of Royal Commission sponsored drug dealer, KX15. I suppose we should at least be thankful that an embargo of sorts was placed on KX15's dealing. He was to deal no more than normal but also no less.

The KX15 operation began quickly and a warrant for a listening device was obtained from Supreme Court Judge, Justice Peter Hidden. The warrant was necessary for the Royal Commission to eavesdrop on conversations that KX15 would have with his clients and his suppliers.

I assume that the Royal Commission was also hoping to hear the voices of corrupt NSW Police chatting with their agent KX15. I am more than curious as to what the Royal Commission used as evidence on the affidavit sworn before his Honour Justice Hidden that referred to police corruption and the link between KX15 and alleged police corruption at Kings Cross. It could not have been any evidence provided by KX15, as he had already been tape recorded as denying his relationship with any corrupt police.

To obtain the warrant, Justice Hidden had to be informed of the basis of which the Wood Royal Commission intended to use KX15. I can only assume that some evidence must have been given to Justice Hidden that KX15 could reveal material about police corruption, as distinct from drug dealing.

Given that KX15 had already denied to Agius and Miller that he had any involvement with police, did the Commission have other material to implicate KX15 in police corruption to provide the basis of the application made to Justice Hidden?

If so, that material has never been publically disclosed in any forum, including in the hearings of the Wood Royal Commission.

Miller said that it has been decided to give KX15's money back. No doubt these were the proceeds of crime from drug sales, commonly an offence known as 'goods in custody'. It is worth revisiting the Drug Misuse and Trafficking Act 1985. Section 3 which includes 'authorising, directing, causing, suffering, permitting or attempting any of those acts or things'.

Just about every adjective in that section was relevant to the Royal Commission's behaviour involving KX15. There was no 'attempt', as the offence actually succeeded.

Was there an offence under Supply, Section 25 (1) if the amount of drugs supplied were within a weight range that made the offence an indictable one? If the amounts or weights of drugs supplied fall under the Commercial Quantity or Trafficable Section of the Act, then the penalties are substantial—some 20 years imprisonment or life for a large commercial quantity.

In the NSW Court of Criminal Appeal in 2000, in *R-v-Bayeh*, the range of offences for Bill Bayeh went from Commercial Supply to Large Commercial Supply of Heroin, and those charges arose from his involvement in the Kings Cross drug trade, in which he acted as a major supplier to KX15.

What quantities of drugs were allowed to be supplied over the period of KX15's Royal Commission role as a protected drug dealer? Did the Royal Commission keep a log or diary of the amounts of drugs KX15 dispensed while he was their witness?

How long did KX15 spread his poison around Kings Cross with impunity? A day or two perhaps?

No. He operated for 25 days, nearly a month. Without labouring the point, you can only guess at the sort of drug quantities that continued to hit the streets through this sanctioned drug dealer.

In the Royal Commission hearings, witness Dominic Pedavoli was examined by John Agius SC about his role in the Kings Cross drug trade. At some point in that examination Mr Agius informed the witness that another Cosmo Cafe 'identity' (KX15) was secretly taping 'all of them' for up to 18 hours a day for weeks—so the 'hours' KX15 appeared to be working were in fact up to 18 hours a day. Going by those hours the quantities of drugs supplied by KX15 would have been extraordinary.

You can only imagine the fallout if the New South Wales Police had sanctioned an operation such as KX15's and it became known to the media, to the government or to the Defence Bar, let alone the Judiciary.

Did it not occur to any of those involved that the risk of overdoses amongst drug addicts is a clear and present danger every time they inject heroin into their veins? Surely someone amongst the police contingent must have seen a fatal drug overdose at some stage of their police careers.

Didn't any of them have reservations about the possibility, not too remote, that an addict could or would overdose on heroin supplied by KX15 and that the supply of that fatal overdose may be tracked back to the Wood Royal Commission?

Between 1992 and 1996, twenty per cent of all heroin-related overdose deaths in the state of New South Wales occurred within the two-kilometre radius of Kings Cross. It was not as though KX15 was being unleashed on a relatively drug free suburb (if one exists now at all), but a suburb where one fifth of all fatal overdoses in NSW was occurring. That statistic alone should have had major implications for the proposed operation. KX15 may have been fitted with a tape recorder, but he was not under constant police surveillance to track his deals and monitor their outcomes.

Whatever the reason, no one appears to have put their hand up and questioned the consequences of a drug supply that goes wrong, fatally wrong.

Just imagine for a moment a case where the NSW Police are conducting a sting on stolen motor vehicles and the re-birthing of those vehicles. They have a stolen car under observation and stop the driver. Now he is in a stolen car. He has clearly committed an offence. But, after due consultation with someone in authority, say at his home during lunchtime, they act on that 'oral advice' and they decide to allow him to drive off in the stolen car to further their investigations.

However, somewhere in his travels the thief again attracts attention of the police, this time the Highway Patrol. A chase begins and ends in a catastrophic fatal accident that kills a family. The driver, as often happens, survives the crash and later tells the courts that the police allowed him to drive off in his stolen car, providing he did what he normally did (drive stolen vehicles) and that he was to report back to them each day.

Manslaughter charges, conspiracy to pervert the cause of justice, aid and abet, negligent act occasioning death—just a few of the sanctions that could be considered in this example, not to mention they would be immediately suspended from duty, paraded before the media at the obligatory Police Integrity Commission (PIC) hearings, later sacked and probably joined as defendants along with the state of New South Wales in a civil court action lodged by surviving family members.

On 21 July 1995, some 23 days after KX15 became a Royal Commission agent, he was going about his daily business of supplying heroin and cocaine to drug addicts in Kings Cross when one of the purchasers complained to KX15 that 'people are dropping in the streets' because of the purity and strength of the heroin he was supplying. What the purchaser appears to be telling KX15 in no uncertain terms is that his customers are overdosing, either fatally or non fatally.

From further documents I have examined it seemed that it caused some degree of panic within the Wood Royal Commission. The thought that heroin, 'hot heroin', had been supplied by their agent KX15 must have sent a shiver down the spine of every person connected with the operation.

'Hot heroin' is an expression normally used by junkies to signify an increased purity or strength in a normal dose or batch of heroin. It is often referred to by authorities as a 'lethal dose' if the addict dies.

There is much debate on what constitutes normal strength for a street heroin deal. For example, the street purity of heroin in Cabramatta was reputedly much stronger than heroin sold around Kings Cross. That can be attributed to the original source of the heroin overseas and the fact that Vietnamese heroin dealers in Cabramatta did not 'cut' down (add other substances to) the pure heroin as much as Kings Cross dealers.

The most powerful heroin is often referred to as No. 4, and is sourced from the infamous Golden Triangle in South East Asia, primarily Burma or Myanmar as it is now known.

Typically, No. 4 heroin is about 80 per cent pure dia-morphine and it is cut down by using substances such as talcum powder, baby food supplements, icing sugar and other easily dissolved powders to 'bulk' up the heroin deal. It may be cut down up to seven or eight times from its original purity before it ends up in the veins of a heroin addict.

However, there have been studies that show 'street level' purity of heroin seized to be anywhere as high as 60 per cent in Cabramatta. Reports of 8-10 per cent purity were typically found in and around Kings Cross in 1995 and 1996.

There were certainly significantly more heroin overdoses in Cabramatta all through the 1990s than anywhere else in Australia. Of that there is no doubt. Whether increased purity was responsible or whether it was just the sheer numbers of junkies that descended on Cabramatta on each and everyday of the year.

The age and experience of an individual heroin addict doesn't seem to make that much of a difference in terms of their vulnerability to an overdose. Just as many older experienced users die from lethal doses of heroin as do the younger less experienced users. But addicts that use frequently do build up a tolerance for heroin that requires them to use greater amounts more often to satisfy their cravings.

When the balloon went up at the Royal Commission over the 'hot heroin' incidents, it appears that the investigators either panicked or took swift action, according to whose recall of events you wish to believe. Investigators from the Wood Royal

Commission raided Cosmo's with the specific aim of seizing hot heroin. Which begs the question, how did they know which heroin was hot?

At that time another very interesting conversation took place between Kieran Miller and KX15 which was recorded on tape and subsequently admitted as evidence in the trial of KX15's criminal associates:

> *Miller: I understand the position you're in, but you've got to understand the position we're in. We cannot, you cannot have, any part of selling a drug which you KNEW to have, some prior knowledge which is going to maybe cause an overdose with a person.*
>
> *Now it's just not an option. It's not an option at all. We can't have any part of it. It's called...its basically called Manslaughter.*
>
> *KX15: I swear it's on the tape, I said, 'Peter, somebody's fucking od'd.' I'm shaking like this at him, on tape.*

I can understand why KX15 was shaking; he may have just been implicated in a murder or manslaughter, for all he knew. The following conversation with Kieran Miller must have 'reassured' KX15 that nothing would happen to him courtesy of the original tape recorded agreement with John Agius, nearly three weeks prior.

> *Kieran Miller: Either which way, Peter Kay has to take the drug and he has to get them cut down. You have to recap it; you can't have them one to one.'*

So we have a Royal Commission Investigator, Kieran Miller, telling a mid level drug supplier, KX15, to tell his supplier, the heroin wholesaler, Peter Kay, how to control the purity and strength of his heroin. Doesn't that fall within the meaning of 'authorise, encourage', as in the legal definition of 'to supply heroin'?

And so, after receiving information from their 'agent' that he has just supplied 'hot heroin' to his customers that have subsequently overdosed, Kieran Miller gave a short warning about manslaughter and then instructed KX15 to get his supplier to cut down the strength of the street heroin, obviously with a view of the heroin supply operation continuing.

As I have written previously, this whole operation should never have taken place but once it was underway, it should have been closed down the minute it became apparent that an addict or addicts had overdosed.

Significantly, the conversation above reveals that Miller was concerned that manslaughter charges could have arisen as a direct result of the supply of hot heroin to addicts by the Wood Royal Commission's operation.

The conversation also reveals that Miller directed KX15 to tell his supplier, Peter Kay, to cut down any of the remaining hot heroin to a safer level of purity. What exactly is a safe level of purity? Under whose instructions did this quality control measure originate from?

Why didn't someone at the Wood Royal Commission to pull the plug on this highly controversial operation before more addicts dropped in the streets? Was there not a duty of care owed by the Royal Commission towards potential victims of this sting?

There was an element of foreseeability both before the operation with KX15 commenced and even more so after the hot heroin incident. With no evidence of police corruption, when the hot heroin incident became known to the Royal Commission, the support of KX15 should have ceased, along with his operations.

How did the Royal Commission trust KX15 to tell his supplier Peter Kay to cut down the heroin to a weaker purity? What if he didn't and further overdoses resulted?

The Royal Commission officers did seize 60 caps of supposedly hot heroin from a raid on Cosmo's. But from that one raid they could not have been certain that all hot heroin was off the streets.

What followed the day after the hot heroin raid on Cosmo's Cafe perhaps answered the perplexing question of who within the Wood Royal Commission knew of the sanctioned heroin dealing by KX15. On 22 July, 1996 a packed Royal Commission hearing room heard this amazing and I say, unprecedented address, firstly from John Agius, Counsel Assisting and then His Honour, Justice Wood:

John Agius: Mr Commissioner, last night officers of the Royal Commission executed a search warrant on the Cosmopolitan coffee shop in Darlinghurst Road, Kings Cross. During the course of the search a large number of caps of heroin were seized. There has been a preliminary analysis of that heroin, which leads officers of the Royal Commission to have grave concern concerning the heroin.

The analysis information that we have indicates that that heroin was three to four times the usual strength or purity of heroin found in caps on the street in Kings Cross, sometimes in the order of 30 percent plus, whereas caps more often found on the street run between eight and ten percent.

Information available to the Royal Commission from medical experts suggests that caps of heroin running to 30 percent plus are likely to be lethal, even in the hands of experienced heroin users. It is very likely that there are other caps of this same heroin either on the street at the moment or likely to come on the street in the next short time and it is important that a warning go out in the strongest and loudest possible terms to even experienced heroin users to be aware. These caps are completely indistinguishable from other caps of heroin to the eye and indeed, physical examination without analysis of the heroin will not put the user on notice.

We have all heard of recall notices about contaminated groceries from department stores, but I have never heard of a heroin recall. What John Agius did not go on to say to the large media throng present, was that the recall was mostly sponsored by the Wood Royal Commission, who were in part, responsible for this crisis.

The Commissioner, Justice Wood, replied from the Bench:

Thank you, Mr Agius. The reality is that this kind of event happens from time to time and it cannot be predicted in any fashion just how much of the stuff is out there at the moment. It is utterly obscene that anybody should even contemplate placing heroin of that degree of purity on to the streets.

It's time that those who do supply it (heroin) realise that

they are facing a potential charge of murder or manslaughter
if someone dies as a result of it and the heroin can be traced
back to them.

He then continued with another impassioned plea to the victims
or users of the potentially fatal heroin batch:

All I can say is that those who use this substance ought to
be aware of it. If anybody shows any signs of an overdose,
they or those around them should be seeking urgent medical
attention. The relevant hospitals have been notified that
this stuff is about again and I just hope nothing happens to
any young people. I also hope that those who put it on the
street realise just what they are doing to the young people of
this State, particularly if they are parents or have children
related to themselves.

The Royal Commission knew the hot heroin could have been
traced in an instant; the tape-recorded conversation between
Kieran Miller and KX15 the previous evening identified Peter
Kay as the supplier. What more did they need?

Had they arrested Peter Kay on the spot, I have no doubt the
truth would have come out sooner rather than later.

When Peter and Roula Kay later faced the Wood Royal
Commission hearings, were they asked if they had supplied
the hot heroin that was found on the evening of 21 July 1996?
If not, why not?

If the relevant hospitals had been notified, why couldn't
Kings Cross Police or Task Force Bax have been notified as well,
so that they could begin launching murder investigations?

I wonder if the Solicitor General of New South Wales, or Gary Crooke QC, John Agius and other senior members of the Wood Royal Commission, realised what they may have done, through KX15, to the young people of this State. It seems to me at least Justice Wood may have realised that, judging by his language from the bench.

Justice Wood could have ordered an immediate halt to the KX15 operation and ensured that Task Force Bax was notified and allowed to make the arrests which would have taken Cosmo's players out of action for good. He didn't and the debacle continued.

No one from the media appeared to have known or even suspected what was going on under the guise of the Wood Royal Commission. It was one media leak that did not occur.

In an article in the *Sydney Morning Herald* by Chief Police Reporter Greg Bearup on 23 July 1996, two days after the 'hot heroin' incident, Dr Lisa Maher, a university researcher, was quoted as saying that it was odd that Justice Wood would issue a warning for drugs of 30 per cent purity in Kings Cross when on most days in western Sydney drugs of a much higher purity were being sold and a clear distinction had not been made between street level suppliers and organised criminals. Neither the reporter nor the academic would have had the slightest inkling as to why His Honour made this unprecedented address from the Bench.

What responsibility did the Royal Commission have in these circumstances? Surely they would have had the same responsibilities as the NSW Police.

Was an investigation carried out? Was the Commander of Kings Cross Police asked to make discreet enquiries through his officers of recent overdose cases? If not, why not?

If there had been fatal overdose deaths anywhere near the source of supply, then the New South Wales Coroner should have been informed immediately, just as police are required by law in the state of New South Wales to do so.

One crucial question is: how many corrupt cops were caught running off KX15 and Peter Kay?

My information, supported by Court records, media reports, the Commission's own reports and critically, a later District Court judgment by His Honour Judge Vinney, reveals that no police were ever charged as a result of this 'sting'. Not one police officer. Zero.

Judge Vinney remarked in the judgment that not much in the way of naming names of corrupt police had come to light in the trial. Was that a nice way of saying, there weren't any?

What of the oral legal advice that John Agius received from the then Solicitor General of New South Wales? Was the advice given because of the likelihood of police corruption being involved? So would a lack of police involvement in the suspected corruption have still resulted in the approval for the Royal Commission operation to go ahead?

Is the public allowed to examine that advice? No, it is not.

Did that legal advice take into account the foreseeability of potential heroin overdoses?

Judge Vinney in the trial of Peter and Roula Kay for their offences committed with KX15, was never shown the legal advice given to John Agius on 29 June 1996 that allowed this operation to take place. The Crown appears not to have had access to that legal advice either; certainly the defence team was not allowed to view it.

Wasn't the Wood Royal Commission a full and open public inquiry?

Two District Court Judges also had concerns with the KX15 drug supply operation, namely Judges Vinney and Gibson.

Judge Vinney in the trial of Peter and Roula Kay on 9 December 1999 had this to say:

> *It seems to me that knowing a man was a drug dealer...it would be at least improper for people in the position of the investigators and their advisors, to permit and encourage that man to continue with his drug dealing. That is what they did.*

It is interesting that His Honour has included 'their advisors' in the sentence alongside the 'investigators'. That ultimately, may have significance for some, stretching from such hallowed offices such as the NSW DPP, the NSW District and Supreme Courts and even into the highest law court of the land, the High Court of Australia. Who were the 'advisors' on this operation? The public has a right to know.

Crucially His Honour uses two of the words needed to prove the 'supply' of heroin under the Act: 'permit and encourage'. If you read that extract again, the proofs of supply seem to have been outlined by His Honour and it included not only the investigators, but more importantly, 'their advisors'. His Honour goes on:

> *I have had some difficulty in determining whether [WRC staff] has committed an offence. [The Defence] argued that they were aiding and abetting KX15 to deal in drugs. Against*

that, there is the clear evidence...that but for the interception of KX15 by the [WRC] KX15 would have continued to sell drugs, and if they took him out of the Cosmo situation, the drug suppliers would have replaced him with someone else, so nothing would have been gained.'

With great respect to His Honour, Judge Vinney, we will never know whether KX15 would have been replaced by other dealers if he had been 'taken out' by Wood Commission staff on the 29 July 1996.

It is likely that the suppliers would have put in another dealer to take KX15's place but then again, the arrest of KX15 may have made the suppliers wary, for at least a short time, of continuing this operation. It may have also, critically, altered the 'hot heroin' incident.

His Honour then delivered what I think to be critical comments on KX15's drug supply operation and the involvement in that of the Wood Royal Commission:

My view is that the participation of [WRC staff] in using KX15 to record his conversations with the Kays and Bayeh and others while he continued to peddle drugs was actually illegal. If not strictly 'illegally' it was at least improper from a legal perspective.

Why weren't the transcripts and evidence from that trial referred to the Attorney General of New South Wales for him to consider whether the actions of the Wood Royal Commission investigators and their advisors were legal or illegal?

As I was going back over the transcripts of the Judgment

on Remaining Voir-Dire Issues by Judge Vinney QC, dated 9 December, 1999, I came upon something that did not make sense to me. Voir-Dire is an examination of issues held without the jury, during a trial.

It appeared to me, reading those transcripts and backtracking to evidence led by John Agius during the Kings Cross evidence segment in 1996, that in an attempt to ensure that the evidence improperly obtained by the Royal Commission during its operation with KX15 would be admitted in the trials of KX15's criminal associates, the Crown informed Judge Vinney that one of the accused had implicated police in corrupt conduct at that time. This was simply not true.

We have to go back to the day, 21 July 1996, when Task Force Bax made a separate raid to the Wood Royal Commission on Cosmos café and they too seized 60 caps of heroin. The heroin was booked up and entered as an exhibit and was later analysed and properly certified. Everything connected with the raid was completely transparent.

Following the raid, KX15 told Peter Kay that the police have executed and seized 60 caps of heroin. In the conversation that followed, Peter Kay alleges that 'he might be able to get 40 caps back from police' and he gives the name of a police officer that is apparently connected with Task Force Bax. The allegation was fantasy and more likely made by Peter Kay to boast to KX15 that he had high connections in the New South Wales Police, as crooks of all persuasions are prone to do. It's called lifting their weights, enlarging their profile amongst other criminals, where police connections are always an important part of a crook's CV, even though 99 per cent of the time it is plainly untrue.

The Wood Royal Commission took the allegations of the

connections seriously and mentioned it in the Commission hearing rooms prior to Peter and Roula Kay being called to give evidence. The 'allegation' then advanced to the point where a 'secret New South Wales Police Task Force' had been 'compromised'. Although Task Force Bax was not mentioned by name, the allegation was sufficient enough for it to achieve perhaps what it was intended to do—to cast a cloud of doubt over that New South Wales Police unit. This was reported in the *Sydney Morning Herald* the day after the hearings by Kate McClymont.

While the Wood Royal Commission could find no evidence of police corruption linked with their agent KX15's drug operation, Peter Kay's boast was seized upon to make their suspicions look well founded. The only way to get that into the public domain was to allow an unsupported and untested allegation to find it's way to an unsuspecting media to be plastered over the morning newspapers.

It also appears that the allegations lingered far, far longer than just the next day's newspapers. In fact, as referred to previously, it was used by the Crown years later as a submission for ensuring that the evidence that the Crown had to rely upon in the trial of KX15's associates was admitted, notwithstanding that it had been improperly obtained.

The allegations about police officers were not only false, but demonstrably so, once Peter Kay was questioned in the witness box by John Agius and asked about his recorded conversation with KX15. Peter Kay immediately confessed that he had made it up.

John Agius: Have you ever had dealings with corrupt police officers?

Peter Kay: No, I haven't.

John Agius: You've never had a corrupt relationship with a police officer?

Peter Kay: No, none whatsoever.

John Agius: Have you ever had access to sources of information, that is, sources of confidential information from within the Police Service?

Peter Kay: No I have not.

John Agius: Have you ever had anybody who is not a police officer who has passed on confidential information to you which you believe to have come from the Police Service?

Peter Kay: From memory, no I haven't. I've never had anything to do with informants of the police force.

John Agius: You've never been tipped off about a raid?

Peter Kay: No.

John Agius: Or a search?

Peter Kay: No.

John Agius: Ever?

Peter Kay: No.

John Agius: Did you ever have any expectation that any of the drugs which were found in the safe of the Cosmopolitan cafe on the day that the search warrant was executed by New South Wales Police, that any of those caps or drugs would come back to you?

Peter Kay: Did I have any expectation that they would? No I didn't have any expectation that they would.

John Agius: Did you ever hope that they would come back to you?

Peter Kay: No, I didn't.

John Agius: Did you have a relationship with a police

officer which gave you reason to believe that some of those drugs might come back to you?

Peter Kay: I've never had any relationship with any police officer in New South Wales, or any other state for that matter.

John Agius: Have you ever passed yourself off as being a person who has relationships with corrupt Police?

Peter Kay: No.

John Agius: Never?

Peter Kay: No.

John Agius: To anybody?

Peter Kay: Not from memory, because I've never had a relationship with any police officer at all. Sometimes we talk a lot of nonsense when in the company of friends. I can't recall saying anything like that.

Peter Kay is continually asked about his 'alleged' relationship with corrupt police, which he denies over and over and over again, never backing down from the fact that he does NOT know any police, isn't friends with any police and had never paid police any money. But neither John Agius nor Justice Wood appears to want to give in:

John Agius: We are investigating why you were never raided, Mr Kay. Surely that point has not been lost upon you?

Peter Kay: I don't know why we were never raided, Mr Agius. I can't answer that.

John Agius: Were you not raided because you were paying money to Police not to raid you?

Peter Kay: I have never paid any money to any Police if you are suggesting something like that.

Justice Wood: Let's be plain about who's paid money and we will return to your so called partners. To your knowledge, have any of your partners or associates in this business [been] paid money to police?

Peter Kay: I've never seen any of my business partners or associates pay money to Police, commissioner.

Justice Wood: The facts as you say, you've run the place for eight years, you've had no raids, no drugs found in there until a few weeks ago, when every time a law enforcement agency has gone there in the last few weeks they've found drugs?

Peter Kay: That's correct.

Then supposition reared its head as the unsuccessful questioning of supposed police corruption continued.

Justice Wood: Do you think you were unwittingly or unknowingly receiving protection?

Peter Kay: Well, I personally couldn't have been receiving any protection because I've never had anything to do with any police officers or any other body, for that matter, or paid out any money in order to receive protection.

Unwittingly or unknowingly receiving protection? Peter Kay had already answered dozens of questions relating to the 'apparent' corrupt relationship he had with police, now that relationship was perhaps, an unwitting or unknowing one. It appears to me the Wood Royal Commission had realised that they had a problem with this witness, he was either not telling the truth or he was and he did not have any improper or corrupt relationships with NSW Police. That might be good news for some, but not for the Wood Royal Commission, which had embarked on the KX15 drug supply operation on the very basis that there was corruption in Kings Cross surrounding heroin dealing.

The questions continued, but without the usual 'guillotine' scenario, where witnesses were led in evidence, supposedly lying to the Commission and then a star witness appears and discloses the lies of the witness, who later returns to the witness box and confesses all.

John Agius: So you say that none of your partners or associates have ever been seen by you to pay police?

Peter Kay: That's correct.

John Agius: Have they ever spoken to you about making payments to Police?

Peter Kay: No, they have not.

John Agius: Have they ever given you information in the nature of a tip off that a police raid might be forthcoming?

Peter Kay: No, they have not.

John Agius: What about when you were working at Illusions? Did you ever receive tip offs then that the police might be about to execute a warrant or that they might be about to undertake a raid.

Peter Kay: There were never any warrants executed- no, I was not. Sorry, I will be direct with my answers now. No.

John Agius: That never happened.

Peter Kay: No.

John Agius: Let me just cover one or two points with you. You say you've never had a corrupt relationship with any police officer?

Peter Kay: Never.

John Agius: Never done a corrupt deal with a police officer?

Peter Kay: Never.

John Agius: Never sought to do one?

Peter Kay: Never.

John Agius: You have never paid a police officer any money for some corrupt advantage?

Peter Kay: Never.

John Agius: And never offered to do it?

Peter Kay: Never.

John Agius: You've never been tipped off or provided with information to which you were not entitled by a police officer?

Peter Kay: Never.

At this point, the proceedings are stopped and Peter Kay is told that KX15 has been a covert operative for the Wood Royal Commission and has been tape recording him for a number of weeks.

This typically would be the point where, if Peter Kay had been doing business with corrupt cops, he would have confessed to save his own skin.

Peter Kay is sent with his lawyers to a small room within the Commission building to have a rethink of his evidence. After a brief time he re-emerges and goes back into the witness box.

John Agius: Mr Kay, would you accept from me that later evidence will disclose that Gary Said (KX15) has in fact been working as a covert operative for many weeks now?

Peter Kay: Yes I realise that.

John Agius: And that many of your conversations with him have been recorded?

Peter Kay: Yes I understand that.

John Agius: Would you accept from me that many of those conversations record you deep in talk about drug dealing with him?

Peter Kay: Yes, I would accept that.

John Agius: Mr Kay what is your position at the moment? Are you of a mind to cooperate with the Royal Commission and truthfully answer questions that are put to you?

Peter Kay: Yes, I will.

John Agius: Have you ever had dealings with corrupt police officers?

Peter Kay: No, I haven't.

John Agius: You've never had a corrupt relationship with a police officer?

Peter Kay: No, none whatsoever.

Peter Kay is now a co-operative Commission witness. He has admitted his involvement in drug dealing with the Royal Commission's own drug dealer KX15 and he would, I suggest, at this time, be looking for 'an ace out of the pack', or a get out of jail card, because that is where he is heading. That ace would have been the details of a corrupt police officer and Peter Kay would almost certainly had known from the book of questions thrown at him about alleged corrupt associations with police, that that is what the Royal Commission wanted.

Unfortunately for both Kay and the Royal Commission, he couldn't deliver, because there were no corrupt police in Peter Kay's operation.

From the numerous hours that KX15 taped Peter Kay and their drug dealing, only one claim of police corruption was ever mentioned and that was an invention on the part of Peter Kay to lift his profile in KX15's eyes. It was a fantasy.

John Agius: Well, would you listen to this tape, please? This was recorded on 10 July, 1996. This is the day after the execution of the search warrant upon the Cosmopolitan, when 60 caps were found in the safe...

Did you hear yourself say words to the effect '40 will come back if...got them?'

Peter Kay: Yes.

John Agius: Who were you talking about?

Peter Kay: I was only big noting myself. I've never met...... until the other day when there was a raid and I met him for the first time. I was only big noting myself to Gary (KX15), because he always tends to do that. I was only getting back at him.

Further on Peter Kay explains it again.

...I recall this conversation but. .....I never met till the other day when there was a raid at the Cosmo. I rang up the Cosmopolitan and he said who it was.

John Agius: Why pick on in particular ..?

Peter Kay: I think Gary might have said that was the

officer-in-charge and I said that to him. I can't remember how...(His) name came out of this to be honest with you.

The only mistake the officer made, was simply to answer a phone call from Peter Kay and identify himself to him as you are required to do in a search warrant situation. That is all he did. Yet he was initially named in hearings, and advised that he had been adversely named, albeit, by a drug dealer. I have suppressed his name because he is innocent and doesn't need the association of the allegation aired again.

Peter Kay had ample opportunity to name and shame a corrupt police officer, if there was one. He didn't and he couldn't. There was no one to name.

The detective who was wrongly accused was never called to the Royal Commission. He was never asked to formally respond to the initial allegations by Kay. It was untrue from beginning to end and it was proven to be by John Agius in front of His Honour Justice Woods during the interrogation of Peter Kay.

So how did this allegation become repeated in a District Court and in fact get given some recognition, albeit, mistakenly, by a District Court Judge?

An even more prominent player, Bill Bayeh's brother Louis Bayeh, was caught on Bax listening devices continually telling KX15 that he will support his dealers except for one, very critical thing:

Louis Bayeh: One thing I can't support you... I can't ... I don't nothing with the cops.

KX15: You let me look out for my own problems with the Police.

But KX15 didn't have any problems with the Police because he had the might and power of the Wood Royal Commission behind him.

> *Louis Bayeh: With Police I don't do fucking business.*
> *With anyone I do business… the police I don't do business.*
> *I hate fuckin' coppers. I don't do business with no coppers. I hate them, I hate them. You know that yourself.*
> *KX15: I know that.*

In this tape recording KX15 is captured boasting like Peter Kay:

> *KX15: I'll do the fuckin business with the police. I've come, I..I..*
> *Louis Bayeh: Whatever you do with Police, your business. I don't wanna know.*

During the further conversations between Louis Bayeh and KX15, Bayeh mentions another six times, how he won't do business with Police, hates them, doesn't trust them etc.

Louis Bayeh was a major organised crime figure in the Kings Cross underworld, far, far bigger than Peter Kay or KX15. So who were the police that John Agius and the Wood Royal Commission suspected of corrupt involvement in the Kings Cross drug trade?

The suspicion was obviously strong enough for them to go to the New South Wales Solicitor General and organise an unprecedented drug operation that came off the rails with the hot heroin incident. The public should know that much, because I have begun to suspect the Wood Royal Commission may have had no evidence, other than mere suspicion, when they went before the Solicitor General of New South Wales to get advice about running KX15.

There was another startling allegation by Peter Kay against KX15 that may also have had some repercussions had the issue been taken further.

John Agius: Mr Kay, when Mr Bill Bayeh was arrested, do you still say that Mr Said (KX15) was putting pressure on you to supply him with drugs?

Peter Kay: Not as much putting pressure, but he wanted to keep going so he could make some money. Otherwise he said he was going to give us all up.

Justice Woods: He said otherwise he was--?

Peter Kay: Going to give us all up, dob us in.

John Agius: Do you say if he hadn't said that to you, you wouldn't have continued to provide drugs?

Peter Kay: Well, I had considered not continuing, yes.

Whether Peter Kay was serious in divulging that he had considered giving up supplying drugs is irrelevant. What is relevant is whether KX15 'encouraged' Peter Kay to continue in the supply of heroin.

Obviously KX15 didn't want his dream run to end too early and I suspect that the Wood Royal Commission wanted him to keep going too, waiting for that elusive corrupt police officer.

So who was supplying who in these circumstances? Was KX15 just merely the street dealer and Peter Kay the intermediate supplier, or was Peter Kay just a source for KX15's successful operation. I couldn't quite work it out. It must have been that Peter Kay was the main player as that was reflected in his sentence at the District Court a few years after this.

Peter Kay never had corrupt involvement with police, neither did KX15 and neither did the major underworld player Louis Bayeh. Now I am not suggesting for one moment that corruption didn't exist in the NSW Police Force at this time nor am I suggesting that the Wood Royal Commission did not find corruption in Kings Cross. But the only words of possible corrupt conduct that related to police involvement in the drug trade that concerned the KX15 operation was a 'boast' by Peter Kay, nothing else.

Even though the Wood Royal Commission was obliged to follow up the boast by Peter Kay, the amount of questioning by both Justice Wood and John Agius persisted, when Peter Kay robustly denied any involvement in corruption, but readily admitted his drug dealing.

Interestingly, there was not a single shred of any evidence to support his boast throughout the entire 25 day period of recorded conversations with KX15.

That should have been the end of that allegation, and dispelled any rumours of corrupt police feeding off heroin dealers, specifically those associated with KX15.

At the trials of KX15 and his criminal associates in the District Court, the material from the Wood Royal Commission relating to the boast by Peter Kay of police corruption and then the discrediting of that boast, was never presented.

Surely, someone had the transcripts of Peter Kay's evidence before Justice Wood on 25 July 1996. So where were the transcripts? They would have to have been nearby in case the

Defence raised that issue. But I could see no mention of it at all in the transcripts of the trial held before Judge Vinney.

It could be alleged that someone from the Wood Royal Commission staff failed to deliver this vital piece of evidence, because they believed their chances of succeeding in the argument on 'special circumstance' might have been found wanting.

'Special circumstance' under the Evidence Act allows improperly gathered evidence to be admitted at the discretion of the Trial Judge based on submissions justifying the impropriety of that evidence being gathered.

Throw in the police corruption allegation of Peter Kay, based solely on some snippet of conversation with KX15 after the raid, and there is a chance that they would succeed in having the evidence admitted.

Whatever the reasons, the chances of succeeding in the argument of special circumstance would have been severely compromised if the transcript of Peters Kay's evidence before Justice Wood had been available for the defence in those trials. In the absence of that transcript, the discredited police corruption allegation of Peter Kay was not contested and that enabled the evidence obtained improperly by the WRC to be used in the trials of KX15's criminal associates.

Another mystery surrounds the preparation of the briefs of evidence in a number of the matters surrounding KX15. The briefs were prepared by Task Force Bax and police were required to attend each of the trials of KX15 and his criminal associates as witnesses as they had prepared statements and gathered evidence and would most likely be needed for cross examination by the defence.

As in all criminal trials, the police that laid the charges are largely responsible for the day to day running of witnesses and last minute enquiries on behalf of the Crown Prosecutor. Many a week have I spent sitting around a District or Supreme Court running around conducting last minute enquiries on behalf of the Crown. It was just one of the less glamorous parts of being a detective, but a vital cog in the wheel of justice.

However, the detectives in this matter were not required for the duration of the trial of Peter Kay, only the times where they gave evidence. This is very unusual and I was informed by one of the police witnesses that he thought this very odd at the time. It appeared to be that John Agius and perhaps Virginia Bell were doing the 'running around' and not the police.

Had the police been in attendance as evidence was being given, they could have quickly pointed out to both His Honour Judge Vinney and the Crown Prosecutor, John Kiely, that there was an error in the presentation of the evidence relating to Peter Kay and his boast of drugs being returned by supposedly corrupt detectives.

They could have informed the court and His Honour that the allegation of Peter Kay was not only false, but he had recanted it quickly more than three years prior before the Wood Royal Commission.

John Agius gave evidence before Judge Vinney and must have been aware that no police corruption had been uncovered in the course of the KX15 operation. Nevertheless, the Crown in its submission to the District Court wrongly mentioned the allegation of corrupt police involvement that ultimately appears to have had some influence on the Judge in determining the admissibility of the evidence.

There were some other points in Judge Vinney's observations that are worth noting as well. Most importantly, from the aspect of the apparent impunity that Kings Cross drug dealers were operating in, there is mention of the following:

> ...*and there was evidence available to the commission of his (KX15) of his conduct in that he had been selling to an undercover police officer.*

In that short paragraph is evidence that KX15 had been ensnared by Task Force Bax prior to the Wood Royal Commission taking him on as an informer. Nowhere else could I see Task Force Bax mentioned as operating to stop the 'impunity' enjoyed by the rampant drug dealers of Kings Cross. That point too is critical, as going by His Honour's address during Voir-Dire, only the Wood Royal Commission was attempting to halt the rampant supply.

The basis upon which the Wood Royal Commission embarked upon this disastrous operation with KX15 was justified by two reasons. The first was that police corruption had been linked with drug dealing in Kings Cross. There was no evidence tendered, that I could see, anywhere, that supported that view.

The second reason was that 'conventional' means had not worked. That too is debateable, given the earlier success of Task Force Bax in building a brief on KX15 that was ultimately delayed by the Wood Royal Commission when it recruited him.

That drug dealers operated with impunity in Kings Cross does not relate the true position after Task Force Bax began operating. Did anyone from the Royal Commission instruct

John Kiely on the work of Task Force Bax and how it was that Task Force Bax that happened upon KX15, and not, as His Honour mistakenly pointed out, the Wood Royal Commission, in his judgment?

The impunity that His Honour refers to actually occurred while KX15 was running freely around Kings Cross, courtesy of the Wood Royal Commission. His Honour, from the evidence given during the Voir-Dire, also believed that conventional means could not work in the Kings Cross environment. Difficult? Yes. Impossible? No. Task Force Bax proved with the brief they wrapped around KX15 earlier, that it could be done, but that was before the wrapping was stripped off by the Wood Royal Commission.

No one bothered to tell His Honour that a New South Wales Police Task Force had already impugned KX15, long before the Wood Royal Commission got to meet him.

No matter what favourable light you try to shine on the Wood Royal Commissions actions throughout the KX15 experiment, it was, and still is, littered with impropriety.

So the Courts had to rely on the evidence of John Agius when it came to discussing the issue of the legal advice from the Crown Solicitor of New South Wales to Counsel assisting the Wood Royal Commission. The passage from Judge Vinney of the District Court refers specifically to that legal advice:

...He (Agius) said he sought advice from the Solicitor General and still adhered to his opinion...I assume from that that the advice of the Solicitor General was that he approved of this approach. The advice was not written, said Mr Agius and the content was not forthcoming, it having

been declared by earlier judges to be privileged, or so I assume from reading the transcript of the evidence of Mr Agius in the previous trials. It was not raised before me.

His Honour continued with the commentary on the evidence of Counsel Assisting John Agius:

In any event Mr Agius adhered to his view that to allow KX15 to continue selling drugs was not criminal conduct on the part of Mr Agius, nor the Royal Commission investigators: that if he had not been intercepted KX15 would have continued to sell drugs, as he had been doing for years and the Royal Commission were not encouraging that, but merely 'monitoring' his conduct so that they might obtain evidence of corruption by police officers.

This misconstrues the Royal Commission's handling of KX15. KX15 had been intercepted by Task Force Bax and out of strict protocol, the Commander of Bax advised the Counsel Assisting the Royal Commission, Gary Crooke QC, of the serious charges about to be laid on him. The interception of KX15 was 'discouraged' by Counsel for the Wood Royal Commission, in order that KX15 could or would lead the Royal Commission to the doorsteps of police corruption. That, as we know now, never eventuated.

Perhaps the most telling of all the comments in court transcripts is that in Justice Gibson's judgment in the District Court on the 17 August 1998:

I note that no action is contemplated against any of the commission officers who took part in the operation.

At the end of the day, offences appeared to have been committed within the state of New South Wales and the body empowered to investigate and charge is the New South Wales Police Force. Under the new Police Commissioner, Peter Ryan, the guns fell silent and not a single shot was fired off in the direction of the Wood Royal Commission.

Some 12 years later, the High Court of Australia made a decision with lasting implications for law enforcement in Australia. The case concerned Operation Mocha, a controversial drug supply 'sting' involving the secretive New South Wales Crime Commission and directed towards organised crime, that difficult and elusive beast that the Wood Royal Commission also had trouble penetrating.

The controversy surrounding Operation Mocha stems from a decision by the NSW Crime Commission to allow a substantial quantity of cocaine to hit the streets after being detected by them, with the intention of following the trail of the supply and arresting the various dealers.

That appears not to have happened and the drugs circulated around Sydney. One of the Crime Commission's senior staff members, Mark Standen, was involved in this operation and he was later arrested over a separate matter that involved a drug importation allegation that rocked the law enforcement community in Australia.

In a unanimous judgment, the High Court held that controlled operations that involved the selling of large quantities of cocaine to users was conduct 'likely to seriously endanger the health or safety of those people' and should not have been authorised by the New South Wales Crime Commission.

Mocha involved cocaine, which can seriously endanger the health of users. However KX15's operation involved heroin primarily, and that kills people, in fact maybe even 14 people in NSW in that three-week period. If the High Court found the Mocha operation wrong, what would they have said of the KX15 operation?

Peter Robinson, a former solicitor for the New South Wales Crime Commission between 1986 and 1992, was interviewed on the ABC's *PM* program on Radio National, the day the High Court handed down the decision on the Mocha operation. What he explains is not only telling of the Crime Commission's 'sting operation', but I suspect has implications certainly for the Wood Royal Commission KX15 scandal:

> *That is that the use of an undercover operative and the physically supplying of cocaine to these people, so that they could basically obtain evidence of criminal activity by activity, that in itself is criminal, that that evidence could be excluded in the criminal trial.*

To me the most important part of that paragraph is, 'activity that in itself is criminal'.

Ridgeway's case told them not to engage in this sort of behaviour in 1994, yet the Solicitor General of New South Wales approved of it (apparently) in 1996 and then in 2008, the High Court also said no. Who is right? The High Court in *Ridgeway* and Operation Mocha? Or the Solicitor General of New South Wales and the Wood Royal Commission?

A Royal Commission into a Royal Commission? Has that ever been done before in Australia? Has it been done before within the Westminster system of justice?

Several critics of the action that was taken at that time, such as journalist Steve Barratt, Charlie Lynne, a former army officer and Vietnam veteran and a current member of the Legislative Council in the New South Wales Parliament, former Detective Mick McGann, and myself, to name a few, all believe that the only avenue to find out just how the KX15 scandal began, who knew about it and the aftermath of the 'hot heroin' incident, together with evidence presented in various District Courts, requires an inquiry that has the power to summons witness, subpoena documents and most of all, nullify the 'legal privilege' stumbling block, so that truth can be revealed for all to see. That, we suggest, can only be done by a Royal Commission.

If there were deaths associated with the unregulated supply of heroin, including the 'hot heroin' batch by KX15, under the auspices of the Wood Royal Commission, then the relatives of the deceased should be told. They should be informed that an exercise, designed solely to catch corrupt police in Kings Cross, not only failed to reveal any corruption, but may have led to the regrettable deaths of young Australians, who were simply in the wrong place at the wrong time.

No matter how far down the food chain junkies are, they are still human beings. Their lives may not be worth much in the minds of the general public, but they still exist to the families they leave behind.

I have seen first hand the agony of relatives being informed of a son or daughters death at the hands of a drug dealer and the question always arises, that of whether any drug dealer could be arrested for supplying the poison that killed their child. In 99 per cent of the cases I have dealt with, it is near impossible, yet in KX15's 'hot heroin' incidents, if there were deaths directly attributable to him and his supplier, then the circumstances of that supply, could have fitted into the 1 per cent of deaths that could be linked back to the source.

In 1997, when the Wood Royal Commission began closing its files and the hearings were wound up, intelligence documents and various tapes and film footage was handed back to the New South Wales Police so that further investigations of criminal offences collected during the Wood Royal Commission could be continued.

The task of reviewing some of the tapes and material that the Wood Royal Commission handed back to the NSW Police ironically fell to members of Task Force Bax. Members of the Task Force were already only too familiar with the Kings Cross segment and in particular the activities of KX15.

Amongst that material were the tapes of the listening device that had been gathered during the KX15 Kings Cross operation. As Task Force Bax members began to digest the information, a Bax member, Detective Sergeant Ray Lambie, listened to a startling and ultimately damning tape. What he heard on one of the tapes stunned him. Even as a veteran detective, he could not believe what was on the tape in relation to events of the previous year, 1996.

As Ray Lambie explained later in an interview with Tara Brown of the Channel 9 program *60 Minutes* called *Dirty Work* on 30 March 2003:

> *Well basically the particular tape I was listening to,*

which really raised my eyebrows, was you could hear in the background the door to the cafe opening and someone raced in and said, 'its too strong and we have to cut it down, they're dropping in the streets.

In the same interview with Tara Brown, Superintendent Geoff Wegg, the Commander of Task Force Bax, says he was informed about the interview tapes by Lambie and listened to the tape himself. He said:

Incredulous. We couldn't believe what we were hearing on the tape. It was just so far removed from anything that we expected. It was mind blowing.

Incredulous, definitely, but Task Force Bax members had long suspected that something had not been right with KX15's involvement with the Wood Royal Commission in June 1996.

Geoff Wegg, as the Commander of Task Force Bax, immediately reported the illegalities through the normal lines of communication. Firstly to the New South Wales Crime Commission, then through the Acting Commissioner of Police, Neil Taylor and later through the New South Wales Police Minister, Paul Whelan. Geoff Wegg could not get any of them interested in what had unfolded.

The conversations that both Ray Lambie and Geoff Wegg heard on the Royal Commission tapes appear to have been the critical conversation that first indicated that KX15 had been supplying 'hot heroin' to his customers. To use the words of the person caught on tape: 'they're dropping in the streets'. Addicts were overdosing after buying and using the 'hot heroin'.

The person on the tape, believed to be KX15, has deduced the heroin is too strong and is saying that immediate quality control measures have to be taken.

Steve Barrett, a veteran crime reporter and *60 Minutes* producer, is a master at getting to the truth. The Bar Rat, as he is affectionately known, went to the New South Wales Coroners Office and did his own research into the hot heroin incident at Kings Cross. He was able to find out through the Coroner's records that during that 'mad three week period' as Barrett described, a total of 14 people were reported by New South Wales Police to the State Coroner as having died as a result of drug overdoses. Fourteen Australians died as a result of being supplied with illicit drugs by persons obviously 'unknown' within the State of New South Wales.

It is a staggering piece of information that was endorsed by the Chief Executive Officer of the New South Wales Coroners Court in 2003.

How many died just around Kings Cross? We do not know at this time. But from what I have learnt from my years as a detective is that quite often, addicts will not use immediately near the scene but rather take the heroin with them to inject in privacy and away from detection.

On the other hand, for some the urge to use is so strong they can often only make it a few hundred metres from the point of sale and that is where they usually 'nod off' or drop.

For example, an addict may come from Cronulla by train, purchase drugs at Kings Cross and return home to use in private. Or similarly someone living at say Lithgow or Bathurst or Wagga Wagga may travel to Sydney by car and return with a quantity of drugs to both use and supply around their country towns.

Therefore, the geography of these deaths may be unimportant. It is the time period that these 14 deaths occurred within that really interests me.

I am curious to know whether any meetings took place in the upper echelons of the Wood Royal Commission when the hot heroin first became known. What legal advice was given to Keiran Miller about how to tackle a potential fatal outbreak of hot heroin amongst addicts in Kings Cross?

Neither the New South Wales Police nor the State Coroner would have been aware that these deaths may have been linked to the highly controversial Royal Commission operation. The importance of that notification would have been critical in conducting more thorough toxicology examinations of the deceased addicts with a view to investigating the source of those drugs.

Justice Wood said in a quote taken from a *Sydney Morning Herald* article of 23 July 1996, by Greg Bearup, referring to the Kings Cross 'hot heroin' incident:

> *The comments that were made were subject to the provisions that the drug supplied was in fact known to be of a very high quality and could be tracked back to the supplier.*

The last part of the quote is important. The Royal Commission knew who the suppliers of KX15 were: Peter and Roula Kay and Bill Bayeh. They had ample evidence of Peter Kay's involvement in the making up of the 'hot heroin' which is supported by the advice given to KX15 by Kieran Miller, to tell his (KX15) supplier, Peter Kay, to cut down any of the remaining 'hot heroin' to a safer level.

Both of the proofs that Justice Wood indicated in his quote to Greg Bearup for the consideration of murder or manslaughter charges were coincidentally contained in Kieran Miller's advice to KX15,that the heroin was to strong and too tell the supplier to cut it down.

Had an investigation been carried out immediately by the Royal Commission into these overdoses it would have been very likely that Peter Kay could have been charged with far more serious offences than what he was subsequently charged with before the District Court for his role in the Kings Cross drug supply along with Bill Bayeh.

So was it more important to preserve the integrity of KX15 and the sanctioned drug supply because they hoped to catch corrupt cops in Kings Cross or did an investigation take place into these overdoses?

Task Force Bax began their own investigation, albeit a short lived one. They concentrated on the time KX15 operated on the streets of Kings Cross and began to track the known heroin overdose deaths that occurred in June/July 1996, the critical period in question.

By using the Police Operational Computer System (COPS) Bax members hoped to find the evidence of New South Wales Police reports on what is known as 'located persons', or deaths reported to police and then entered onto the COPS system.

The 'event', as it is called, usually contains details such as time and place of death, circumstances surrounding death, if known and a narrative setting out the facts of the discovery of the body and any witnesses such as friends, relatives or ambulance paramedics that may be called to the scene.

This is exactly what should have been done the moment

KX15 alerted the Wood Royal Commission that the current batch of heroin he was supplying was indeed 'hot'.

Had New South Wales Police been alerted to the spate of heroin overdoses immediately that KX15 advised the Royal Commission, then it is very possible that an investigation could have, as Justice Wood put it, tracked back to the supplier the source of the hot heroin.

Obviously with toxicology tests, witness statements, such as those from KX15 himself along with Royal Commission staff, particularly Keiran Miller and perhaps even John Agius, New South Wales Police could have mounted a very thorough investigation and along with the 'hot heroin' seized by Keiran Miller, I would imagine that a very strong brief of evidence for multiple manslaughter charges, if the addicts had died, could have been levelled against the major supplier Peter Kay and others that were involved.

The fact that Keiran Miller and the Wood Royal Commission were already in possession of at least 60 caps of heroin seized from KX15 would have given the police and the coroner a huge advantage in testing samples from the deceased addicts.

But herein lay a major problem for the Commission. If the hot heroin seized by Keiran Miller and later tested showed the 30 per cent strength that Justice Wood referred to in his address from the bench on 26 July 1996, and could be linked back forensically to the victims of the 'hot heroin' supplied by KX15, then almost certainly KX15 would have been in the dock alongside the suppliers. I am sure that he would have quickly shed his co-operative tag with the Royal Commission to save his skin.

Having been warned off KX15 back in June 1996 by the

Wood Royal Commission, the Task Force did what any old school NSW cops would do. They took out a summons against KX15 and served it personally on a Wood Royal Commission lawyer at the Royal Commission premises. This act of defiance towards the Wood Royal Commission ultimately may have contributed to what occurred next.

As Task Force Bax were beginning to conduct an examination of the former Royal Commission tapes and material relating to the Kings Cross segment, they were raided by members of the Police Internal Affairs Branch. The basis for the raid allegedly surrounded the corruption of one member of the Task Force on a totally unrelated matter to the operations of Task Force Bax. However, for reasons still not clear, Police Internal Affairs raided the entire office and sidelined the entire Task Force.

According to Paul Tuxford, when later interviewed by Tara Brown on *60 Minutes*, it was 'no ordinary raid'. Drawers were turned upside down, lockers removed and many documents seized as a 'result of what later would be described by Police Internal Affairs as not being a raid, but an 'intrusive audit'.

The members of Task Force Bax were then interrogated by Internal Affairs Police and later publicly humiliated before the Police Integrity Commission (PIC) during hearings relating to corruption allegations.

These allegations focussed on one Bax member who had crossed the line. None of the members of Task Force Bax had the slightest, if any, sympathy for the errant Bax member who was now facing corruption charges. Not only had he done the wrong thing and acted corruptly, he had also blackened the name of the highly successful task force, even though the charges were unrelated to his work there.

It was a humiliating experience for the honest, decent members of the Task Force. Their names were circulated freely for the media to work up stories of a supposedly corrupt Task Force that had enormous physical and mental impact on them and their families.

Major health problems affected a few of the Task Force members and their loved ones. One member of the Task Force died as a result of a brain tumour, some in the Task Force believe, brought on by the stress of the Bax scandal.

The media appeared like a pack of hungry sharks at the scene of a shipwreck at the PIC hearings into Task Force Bax.

Many articles were slanted to shame the entire Task Force, and not just the one corrupt officer involved. One of the Task Force members told me of an incident at his local pre-school where he had gone to pick up one of his children. A mother of a child in the same school was also there picking up her child. On seeing him, she glared at him and hurried away with her child even though the kids were in the midst of a conversation about their day at the school.

When I spoke to the Task Force member, you could still see the pained expression and the horror from what happened years before. That was typical of many of Bax members in the aftermath of the media attack on the integrity of all the Bax officers.

Their careers were effectively over after the allegations were aired before the Police Integrity Commission and they became isolated within the confines of the newly formed Crime Agencies command, where it was obvious to them they were not wanted.

Worse was to come for the Task Force Bax Commander,

Geoff Wegg. He was summoned to appear before the Police Integrity Commission hearings to give evidence and then a sensational staged arrest was carried out by members of the Police Internal Affairs Branch before a media throng that just happened to be nearby.

A media-staged 'walk of shame' is a disgraceful strategy that was condemned during the Blackburn Royal Commission. It is interesting to read through that report and see some of the shameful practises heavily criticised by the Blackburn Royal Commission just a few years earlier and compare them with the activities of the Wood Royal Commission during 1995-1997. Was anyone in authority at the Wood Royal Commission at least aware of this heavily criticised practise outlined in Blackburn? For example on page 15 of the Blackburn Royal Commission report, the following is written:

> ..the case against Mr Blackburn was conceived in suspicious circumstances, nurtured on doubtful and insubstantial evidence and born into a world with a fanfare of publicity befitting a lusty offspring and not the weak and sickly creature that arrived bereft of any future.

That paragraph certainly could have been applied to many of the Wood Royal Commission public hearings, where adversely named NSW police officers were walked through the St James Centre, prior to or leaving the Commission hearings, where a waiting media throng put them through the walk of shame. That news footage was replayed over and over again on nightly news programs for their families, including their children, to see. These same children in many instances then had to endure the school yard taunts of having alleged corrupt cops as fathers.

No child deserves that, especially when the alleged evidence against their fathers came from drug dealers, murderers and child molesters.

The Blackburn report goes to the heart of the walk of shame:

> *The sensationalising of the arrest in this way may be acceptable in some countries, but it has no place at all in our community, and the Police must see to it that it does not happen again. It is not a Police function to aid the media in providing entertainment for the public.*

So was it the function of Justice Wood's Royal Commission to entertain the public? The Blackburn report points out on page 22 just what the public perception is when a person is arrested in front of a media pack and attempts to cover his face:

> *Further, it is an insult to human dignity that a man in custody should be held up like the organ grinder's monkey on a stick, for a whole community, in their homes, to despise, before he is even tried. The publication of pictures on TV or in the newspapers of men and women in custody desperately trying to keep their features from public view may give a measure of protection to the publishers against contempt of court proceedings, but such devices merely add to the ultimate humiliation of the captive.*

Who arranged for Geoff Wegg's spectacular arrest at the subsequent PIC hearings? It certainly had the desired impact on attacking the integrity of Task Force Bax and its members. It also certainly had a lasting impact on some of the offenders who had been nabbed by Bax and details of Bax's problems were mentioned in Court by at least one defence lawyer. How different would the criminal world now be, especially in Kings Cross, if these cases had been allowed to continue?

Charges brought against Geoff Wegg in this witchhunt would later be thrown out of court. But not before Geoff Wegg resigned in disgust after 35 years of loyal service to the people of New South Wales and those very people lost one more valuable and experienced police officer.

The single corrupt member of Bax received a custodial sentence for his crimes along with his associate, codenamed J2.

Whether the Internal Affairs raids on Task Force Bax were accidental to the discovery of the KX15 tapes, or whether something more sinister occurred because of the KX15 tapes, will probably be never known. Task Force Bax members maintain there was a definite connection to the discovery of the KX15 tapes and the raids.

Eventually, nearly all members of Task Force Bax resigned and for nearly 10 years waged a battle to undo the injustice that had been done to them. Despite numerous complaints to all of the Labor Government-appointed watchdogs, such as the PIC, the Independent Commission Against Corruption (ICAC), The Ombudsman and the New South Wales Police themselves, the Task Force members never received the justice they sought.

For some years, Task Force Bax's legal team were bounced from one jurisdiction to another as the NSW Government and the NSW Police tried to argue that the Royal Commission was not their problem and any damages sought would not come from them. Eventually this expensive argument was defeated, but not before substantial sums of tax payers money had been wasted by the Police Legal Section and the Crown Solicitors Office on expensive legal counsel.

Eventually there was a victory of sorts for Bax members when their nine-year Supreme Court battle ended in 2008 with the NSW Government and the Police Commissioner settling out of court. But the bitter aftertaste remains.

More importantly, the New South Wales Police and ultimately the citizens of New South Wales, lost 32 detectives with over 500 years of experience and dedicated service between them. You cannot replace that, ever.

Perhaps the final word belongs to the Report to Parliament on Operation JADE, regarding Task Force Bax in 1998. Headed 'Extent of the alleged misconduct', the report went on say:

> *There was no evidence revealed during the public hearings of network based corruption within Task Force Bax or consisting of Bax Officers. Early indications of network based corruption within Bax were investigated but subsequently discounted by the Commission (PIC).*

During their long battle to obtain justice, members of BAX made a number of complaints to various oversight bodies with little success. Eventually the highly regarded *60 Minutes* program took an interest and a segment called *Dirty Work* was broadcast in March 2003 and despite the allegations made during the program, it attracted little media and political attention.

Bax members' complaints to ICAC resulted in a lengthy letter being prepared and signed off on by the then Commissioner of

ICAC, Irene Moss. Several members of Bax took exception to various assumptions and errors that were contained in the correspondence and one member wrote back to Irene Moss and received a reply indicating that a far as the ICAC were concerned the matter was finished, there would be no further investigations.

The letter from ICAC was later made available to members of Task Force Bax through the New South Wales Police Legal section and it makes interesting reading. Interesting, because no member of Task Force Bax was ever interviewed by ICAC following the lodging of the complaint against members of the Wood Royal Commission. Why were they not interviewed?

ICAC's 'investigation' appears to have consisted of corresponding with the Wood Royal Commission, watching the video of the *60 Minutes* story, and reading through court transcripts and a few court judgments. ICAC also, apparently, examined the relevant communications in regard to John Agius's legal advice from the Solicitor General. It was listed by ICAC as, 'written communications to and from the WRC'.

The question still remains, where is the written legal advice given by the Solicitor General of New South Wales in June 1996? From everything that I have read in relation to this single issue, I cannot find where anybody in authority, including a number of District Court judges and ICAC, have actually viewed the document and its contents. Is the 'written communication to and from the WRC' the extent of this legal advice? Or did the Solicitor General of NSW prepare and endorse written legal advice?

There appears to have been no interviews conducted with any of the Royal Commission staff involved in KX15's case.

Why not? How do you conduct an investigation without talking to anyone?

The heading of the report refers to allegations regarding alleged corrupt activities of Police Royal Commission staff. Is that not sufficiently serious enough for a wide ranging investigation? The letter from Moss and ICAC, seems more of a review of material as opposed to an investigation of complaints made by former police.

There are various assumptions, suppositions, errors of fact and contra allegations of criminal conduct against Bax members in the ICAC letter. Had Task Force Bax members been interviewed, I doubt any of the above errors and assumptions would have found their way into the correspondence. ICAC says in their letter:

> *According to assertions made in the* 60 Minutes *program, before KX15 agreed to co-operate with the WRC, Bax had KX15 'under constant surveillance, had a number of video recordings of him 'selling drugs' to an undercover cop, were 'about to nail him' and regarded it as very important to get him off the streets.*

ICAC got that right. Every single one of those assertions is based on fact and had ICAC left the precincts of the Sydney CBD and interviewed members of Task Force Bax and perhaps even the *60 Minutes* producer, Steve Barrett, they would have found out that:

1. Bax had informed Senior Counsel at the Wood Royal Commission that they intended to arrest and charge KX15

almost immediately with serious drug offences;

2. Task Force Bax was directed by a Senior Counsel from the Wood Royal Commission NOT to touch KX15;

3. Task Force Bax were very concerned about KX15 being allowed back on the street with a brief hanging over him;

4. They certainly did have a number of lawfully obtained recordings of KX15 dealing in drugs from Cosmo's;

5. KX15 did sell to an undercover cop.

Most importantly, a summons for drug offences by KX15 was provided to a Royal Commission lawyer. Had ICAC checked KX15's criminal history, they would have seen that a summons was issued on a certain date and who the police informant was.

All that ICAC needed to do was interview Task Force Bax members and the assertions would have been verified. The correspondence went on to conclude that: 'No explanation is provided why Bax had not already arrested KX15.' Again, had Bax members been spoken to, an explanation certainly would have been provided.

The paragraph that angered everybody that read the ICAC correspondence was this:

Whomever the 'undercover cop' was, presumably a member of Bax he or she was undoubtedly committing a criminal offence by purchasing the drugs from KX15.

This is somewhat ironic given the allegations against staff of the WRC in relation to KX15.

Compared to the volume of drug trafficking carried out by KX15 under the WRC operation, the low quantity of monitored and booked up drugs purchased by the Bax officer does not deserve to be characterised by ICAC in this way.

Besides, Bax had a lawfully obtained listening device granted by a Justice with the express purpose of proving heroin supply by KX15 in Cosmo's. This is where the report appears to begin to show a slight agenda, playing semantics in defending the Royal Commission but criticising Bax.

A warrant for the use of a listening device by KX15, whilst engaged in drug dealing, was granted by Justice Hidden of the NSW Supreme Court. It follows that it may be assumed that Hidden J was informed of the details of the proposed KX15 operation and that he did not find them objectionable.

Did the ICAC interview Justice Hidden and ask him whether the Royal Commission staff that swore an affidavit before him, disclosed the proposed operation in its 'entirety' including the continuing supply of heroin by KX15? I would be surprised if he was made aware of that proposition. I have sworn out a number of listening device applications before Supreme Court Judges. In my wildest dreams I cannot imagine informing a Justice that I had an informant that I wanted to continue to supply vast amounts of heroin in the 'hope' that I might capture his supplier during the operation. Surely the proposition that 'corrupt police' might be involved throws out all legal principle connected with the granting of a Listening Device Warrant.

The huge difference in both the Wood Royal Commission and Bax was that the drugs connected with Bax were filmed, identified, analysed and booked up as an exhibit and later formed part of the brief of evidence.

The Royal Commission drugs, except for the 'hot heroin' sold by KX15 between 29 June and 24 July 1996, were not booked up, because there was, unlike Bax, no control over them. Did that not occur to the ICAC when conducting their investigation of the complaints by Bax? Another quote from the letter:

> ... On *the* 60 Minutes *program no explanation was offered for why Bax waited until 15 months after the KX15 operation had concluded to make its complaint against WRC staff involved in that operation.*

Had Task Force Bax members been interviewed and a review done, then it would have come to light that Bax did not receive the confirmation tapes of KX15 from the WRC for 15 months, almost to the day. The WRC divested most of its intelligence holdings and evidence not used in the WRC hearings after the Wood Royal Commission came to an end. It took 15 months for the tapes to arrive, to be monitored by Bax staff and the illegality or impropriety to be discovered by rather stunned Bax members. Within three days of becoming aware of the KX15 sting I am advised that complaints were made to the Acting Commissioner of Police, Neil Taylor and to the New South Wales Crime Commission .

The final paragraph of the ICAC correspondence says it all, as far as Bax members were concerned, and led them to believe that ICAC was not serious in their investigation of their complaints:

Overall, it is the Commission's firmly held view that the assertions made on the 60 Minutes program do not stand up to the facts. Indeed it would seem that those responsible for putting the story together failed to conduct even the most basic of research into the allegations. Had they done so, even material freely available in the public domain, it is difficult to think that the story would have been presented in the manner and way that it ultimately was. The allegations are so unmeritorious as to lead one to be suspicious of the circumstances surrounding their making.

Had ICAC spoken to Bax members, they would have been informed that Bax took out a Local Court summons for the serious drug matters on KX15 in the days following his release by Senior Counsel for the Wood Royal Commission and that summons was handed directly to a Wood Royal Commission lawyer. Perhaps that alone should have satisfied ICAC Commissioner Ms Moss and her staff that Task Force Bax did all they could in the circumstances, they did everything according to the law when investigating KX15 and it was no fault of theirs that the drug dealing in Kings Cross did not APPEAR to be getting any better at that time.

A member of Bax was so outraged by the errors contained in the ICAC review/report that he wrote a strongly worded, yet logical defence of Bax and the 'assertions' made. They included the critical issues I have covered in the above paragraphs concerning:

1. The timing of Bax's complaints on the illegality or impropriety of KX15 drug supply.

2. The 15 months it took for Bax to receive the WRC tapes

which alerted them to the activities of WRC staff and
KX15.

3. The fact that they were instructed to 'cease and desist' by
the WRC over the charging of KX15 prior to 29 June 1996.

4. Who in authority Bax complained to, without success,
over the WRC/KX15 operation.

5. And, what they believed to be the current available
evidence of serious misconduct, if not criminal offences,
connected with the KX15 operation that may also have
extended to Perjury in subsequent trials in the District
Court.

The controversy over the KX15 drug supply and Task Force
Bax remains unresolved with little hope that they will ever
be. Justice in New South Wales is not blind but very short
sighted when the circumstances require it to be. When former
police sought justice over the Wood Royal Commission and it's
mistakes, they encountered the full might and financial backing
of the State of New South Wales. Would it have not been easier
and less costly to simply hold an inquiry into the claims?

Many of these disaffected former police are adamant that
there has been a massive cover-up. Who is hiding what and for
whom?

The Police Integrity Commission took over certain
requirements of the Wood Royal Commission following its
final report. I and other police found puzzling the appointment
of His Honour Justice James Wood QC as the Inspector of the
Police Integrity Commission. In the case of disaffected police
such as those from Bax, and the KX15 saga, did anyone consider
that a complaint by them against the Royal Commission may

have put His Honour Justice Wood in an unenviable position?

How could they go to the Inspector of the PIC to ask for a review, when His Honour was the Commissioner of the Royal Commission? I don't suggest for any moment that His Honour Justice Wood would not have done what was right if those circumstances had prevailed. But what plans were made when the government, presumably the Attorney General of NSW, made this announcement?

The ramifications of the Task Force Bax saga continue to this day. Some of the criminals prominently in the media in 2009 over shootings and alleged bikie connections, were identified by the Bax team in 1996. One high profile example is Hassam (Sam) Ibrahim, one of the Ibrahim brothers, who was charged in 1997 with drug offences. However, the prosecution case against him collapsed, primarily due to the adverse publicity generated during the PIC hearings. The Ibrahim brothers were involved in 2009 in the shooting of one of their family members on Sydney's north shore.

That leaves the question raised in his submission in 2003 about the Wood Royal Commission aptly titled, 'Who guards, the guards?' by former Detective Mick McGann: *does anybody know?*

3.

THE KAREELA

CAT BURGLAR

If the story of KX15 doesn't raise enough questions about the investigative integrity of the Wood Royal Commission, then the case of John Harvey Rider, codenamed YN1, certainly adds to that number. It stands as an example of the way in which the WRC mismanagement of an investigation led to five decorated senior policemen becoming enemies of the state.

This story has its origins way back in 1984 in the sleepy southern Sydney suburb of Kareela. It was a typical middle class family neighbourhood and crime, even in the 1980s, had not really begun to become an issue, certainly nowhere near as much as it had in western and southwestern Sydney.

All that changed with the arrival of a man known as the infamous 'Toorak Cat'. John Rider was a highly successful sneak thief, break and enter merchant and career criminal from

Victoria, even though he had reputedly attended a prestigious Victorian private school.

For the purposes of this chapter we will refer to him by his Wood Royal Commission code name, YM1. He earned this codename as he, like the informant KX15, was granted special status as a Commission witness.

YM1 had one of the most vile and despicable reputations that I have come across in my police career. I did not meet him, of that I am thankful, but I have mates in the New South Wales Police that did, much to their detriment.

In 1959, in his late teens, YM1 was carrying about his usual practise of breaking into premises at night using stealth and the darkness to commit daring robberies on unsuspecting Victorians as they slept peacefully in the secure world of their own homes. Or so they thought.

Frequently YM1 would strip naked and even hose himself down to make himself wet so that he could slide through the narrowest of openings to gain entry late at night into residential homes. There he would stand undetected at the foot of his victims' bed as they slept, sometimes even responding to them when they asked who was there in the pitch dark. He was reported to have told one victim it was their son and he was home and for them to go back to sleep.

Young children often awoke in the middle of the night to have this freak standing at the end of their bed staring at them. You cannot begin to imagine the trauma that this must have caused a number of young children in their formative years.

That same year, YM1 committed what was to be ultimately his most vile and despicable act and one for which, he should still be serving a prison sentence in 2009.

He broke into a hospital in the Melbourne suburb of St Kilda and found himself in the maternity wing where of course a number of babies, just days old, were lying in their cribs. YM1 in an act of absolute and utter depravity placed his penis in the mouth of a newborn baby. I am told that a child of such a young age has a natural instinct to suck and as a result, YM1 ejaculated in the baby's mouth with the result that he or she, began to choke and probably would have choked to death but was stopped by the intervention of a night sister on duty.

Disturbed by the night sister, YM1 ran from the scene but was later identified and arrested by fingerprints he left behind at the hospital. He learnt quickly that leaving fingerprints at crime scenes was a big mistake.

When he was arrested YM1 alleged that he received a hard time from the Victorian police. He received a prison sentence that was not long enough and when released he continued his career as a master cat burglar.

In the early 1970s he terrorised the affluent Melbourne suburb of Toorak. He told arresting police that he committed between 800 to 1,000 robberies, netting over $1 million in proceeds from those robberies.

According to former Detective Mick McGann, who along with Detective Sergeant John Davidson would later charge YM1 in New South Wales, so well did the 'Toorak cat' plan his robberies that he even parked his vehicle at least two miles from the scene as he figured if police set up road blocks, it would only extend to around a two-mile radius. He was amazingly accurate.

Eventually YM1 moved to Sydney, no doubt due to the hard time he allegedly got from Victorian police who continually interrupted his stellar career as a cat burglar and prevented him from preying on more hapless victims.

In 1984, Kareela and the surrounding suburbs became the target of YM1. Soon he was being referred to as the 'Kareela cat burglar' as the residents of the once sleepy suburb began to experience a crime wave involving late night break and enters on their homes while they slept.

YMI's night-time break-ins left many victims traumatised. Many left the area to protect their children. Burglary is far from a victimless crime.

During the period of Commissioner Peter Ryan and the Police Minister Paul Whelan, burglary like many other offences, could be reported by telephone to the Police Assistance Line (PAL) without requiring detectives or uniformed police to attend the scene. Overnight, it virtually decriminalised break, enter and steal and like offences, or so it seemed to detectives.

Burglary can and is a traumatic event for the unfortunate victims and should never have been allowed to be reported merely over the phone for insurance purposes. Many good leads can come from interviewing victims and gaining an understanding of how the crime was committed.

As a young detective in training, I can recall attending numerous break and enter scenes and gaining valuable experience at learning the different methods used by various offenders to gain entry into premises. After looking at crime reports back at the Police Station and comparing the different modus operandi's (MO) used in gaining entry, one began to link offence after offence to individual offenders and when they were eventually caught, that MO would become their signature and multiple offences could then be connected to them.

Through the hard work of local police around Kareela at the time of these burglaries, a modus operandi of the offender began to emerge that it was likely to have been a professional cat burglar. However, the highly trained and experienced members of the Special Breaking Squad in Miranda were not invited to become involved in the case.

Former Detective Mick McGann saw the robbery reports around Kareela growing alarmingly over a short period of time, but neither he nor other members of the Squad could get involved until officially invited to by local police authorities.

Finally YM1's luck ran out and he was arrested by police nearby the scene of one of his break and enters. He had, amongst other property, implements normally associated with burglary offences such as screwdrivers, surgical gloves, a torch and green garbage bags.

When arrested, he gave his name as Joe Pace and his address as Mars. At the police station he was extremely unco-operative and refused to be fingerprinted. He was ordered by the court to remain in custody until his fingerprints were obtained. Given his Victorian Police history, it was easy to see why 'Joe Pace from Mars', aka YM1, was not keen to be identified.

Word of YM1's arrest and his unco-operative attitude soon reached the Major Crime Squad South. The fact that he had only been charged with a small number of offences alarmed the squad, who had been monitoring the crime reports of the night-time break and enters.

Local Detective Sergeant Mick McGann and John Davidson from the Regional Crime Squad South went to the Sutherland Police Station to interview YM1 as he was still yet to be formally identified.

YM1 did not earn his reputation as the 'Toorak cat' lightly. As the detectives were escorting him to an interview room, YM1 leapt ahead and managed to barricade himself in an interview room. He propped a desk against the door and defied all attempts to subdue him. With the risk of escape or using furniture inside the interview room as a weapon to prevent arrest, the use of mace was authorised by Detective Sergeant Brian Harding. Harding was also a Field Supervisor with the then elite New South Wales Police SWOS Unit.

When the mace was released into the interview room, YM1 quickly released his grip on the door and he was subdued. He was then interviewed by John Davidson and Mick McGann and confessed to numerous break, enter and steal offences in the Kareela area from July 1983 until June 1984. He was charged with 61 counts of break, enter and steal, seven attempted break, enter and steal, nine steal motor vehicle, possession of housebreaking implements and assaulting police.

YM1 was formally identified and his criminal antecedents from Victoria were discovered. YM1 not only confessed but also assisted McGann and Davidson in locating a balaclava that he had discarded into bushes near the scene of his arrest. In addition, numerous witnesses identified property that YM1 had stolen from their homes during his crime spree as well as confirming YM1's method of entry into individual premises.

Eventually YM1 stood trial before the District Court where allegations of mistreatment by police were made by Defence Counsel. YM1 was found guilty by a jury and sentenced to 17 years penal servitude by His Honour Judge Harvey Cooper.

YM1 wasted little time after his sentencing to make threats of violence and retribution against the arresting police. He spoke to a reporter after his sentence and said: 'If I can't clear myself through the appeals courts, I'll make Attila the Hun look like the tooth fairy, blood will flow. I'll use violence for the first time in my life to get square.'

YM1's warning to arresting police became somewhat of a prophecy. Some 10 years on, YM1 got to extract his revenge, but not using violence. He used the Wood Royal Commission to do it.

Despite a Court of Appeal throwing out his claims of unfair treatment and fabricated evidence regarding his arrest, and a Police Internal Affairs enquiry also dismissing his claims, the Wood Royal Commission took YM1's claims seriously.

What precipitated the Royal Commission's interest in YM1's arrest was the approach to the Royal Commission by a medically retired former detective.

The detectives that the criminal was alleging mistreatment against included Brian Harding, John Garvey, Mick McGann, John Davidson and Steve York.

The careers of all these detectives could best be described as 'outstanding'. They had confronted many of the state's most violent and resourceful criminals. They had been engaged in deadly shootouts with desperate felons and they were all decorated detectives. Detective Mick McGann was awarded the Valour Medal and Brian Harding held a Queen's Commendation for Brave Conduct.

At least one or two of the Senior Counsel attached to the Wood Royal Commission had acted for clients that had been charged and convicted by these same detectives for major offences, including Conspiracy to Murder and major drug offences.

Brian Harding for instance had arrested, charged and convicted the notorious Sydney criminal George Savvas, who as a result received one of the longest prison sentences handed down in decades for his involvement in a conspiracy to import $220 million of heroin. Savvas had made wild accusations about both Harding and Davidson from the confines of Long Bay prison as he began to languish in a cell for the next 28 years. The allegations were investigated and dismissed by ICAC after notorious Sydney criminal, Arthur 'Neddy' Smith, confessed that Savvas had concocted the allegations and had in fact promised Smith $10,000 to make them on behalf of Savvas.

Savvas would again fall foul of police whilst still in prison attempting to organise a drug importation with other conspirators. He was again convicted and sentenced to a further lengthy term. On the second occasion James Black QC, now a District Court Judge, represented him. James Black QC was also a Senior Counsel attached to the Wood Royal Commission and was the Counsel Assisting in the Kareela Cat Burglar segment of that Commission.

Brian Harding had also been involved in serious cases where another Wood Royal Commission Senior Counsel, Virginia Bell, now a High Court Judge, had acted for an accused criminal named Ledden. Brian Harding had charged Ledden with firearms and drug offences connected with a safe house at Cronulla that was owned by Neddy Smith.

Virginia Bell had worked for the Redfern Legal Service and had represented many controversial criminals.

Two Royal Commission investigators, David McGinlay of the South Australian Police and Philip Stevens of the Queensland Police, were assigned to handle the YM1 investigation into allegations of police brutality.

Philip Stevens had been mentioned during the Fitzgerald Inquiry as having accepted meals and drinks at a premises called Fantasy Photographs which was purportedly a brothel. Stevens at the time was a member of the Queensland Police Licensing branch. Despite this, Stevens was seconded to the Police Royal Commission in New South Wales. It is interesting to note, that the Counsel assisting the Wood Royal Commission was Gary Crooke QC, who had also been the Counsel assisting the Fitzgerald Inquiry where Philip Stevens had been mentioned.

David McGinlay would later resign amidst controversy from the South Australian Police Force in connection with serious disciplinary issues where a number of female police officers appeared in camera to give evidence before an Adelaide Magistrate. McGinlay is now a Private Inquiry Agent in South Australia.

Both Stevens and McGinlay were heavily criticised by a Crown Prosecutor in the course of his consideration as to the issuing of ex officio indictments after the detectives had been found not guilty.

Stevens and McGinlay's actions showed a pattern of false representations to witnesses, coercing witnesses to give statements, compiling statements on behalf of witnesses that did not accord with either the memory of the witnesses or at least was substantially different to the version captured by electronic recording, and with misplacing key evidence and not interviewing witnesses that appeared to be favourable to those detectives involved in the arrest of the Kareela Cat Burglar.

YM1 would also perjure himself throughout this saga and obviously was aiming for compensation sometime down the track if the detectives were discredited; a point not missed by Magistrate Barnett in the committal court proceedings against the five detectives.

In a set up characteristic of the Wood Royal Commission hearings, the detectives were called to the hearing rooms and asked if they maintained their version of events and the evidence given in the Kareela cat burglar trial 13 years previously.

All to a man agreed and they were told to sit inside the hearing rooms as the Royal Commission witnesses were 'rolled in'. The three police rollover witnesses all had one thing in common that was not known at the time to the detectives involved. They had all been visited by McGinlay and Stevens and had been told that other police witnesses had rolled over, when in fact they hadn't.

These witnesses then allegedly told the 'truth' about the events of the arrest. With threats of prison sentences, public humiliation, break up of family structures, loss of their police careers, the witnesses appeared to say what the two investigators from the Royal Commission wanted them to say.

The evidence that these witnesses gave under these threats would later be totally discredited. At subsequent committal proceedings they gave evidence under oath, without the protection of the Wood Royal Commission and their evidence was destroyed by defence counsel.

Several police officers who rolled over and gave evidence were given a codename to protect their identity. There were at least three in this case and they were given the codenames YM2, YM3 and YM4.

Within the confines of the Royal Commission hearing rooms, the Commission asked Detectives Harding, Garvey, McGann and York if they wished to reconsider their position after the evidence of the three rollove' witnesses. They declined.

However, John Davidson couldn't let the moment pass without bringing some old time NSW Police 'reality' back to the Commission hearings. He boldly stepped forward and was ushered into the witness box. The Royal Commission hearing room was electric with anticipation that one of the detectives was about to drop a bombshell. As Royal Commission staff waited excitedly for Davo to begin his evidence, the other detectives who had known him for many years could sort of anticipate what the big fella was about to do, and they were right.

John Davidson, a big man, sat purposely in the witness box, watched intently by His Honour Justice James Wood and Counsel Assisting, James Black QC and the Commission investigators. Word spread around the Commission that one of the legends of the CIB was about to talk in the witness box following the evidence of 'rollover' witnesses. Was this the penultimate moment when the 'old guard' finally caved in?

As John Davidson composed himself, His Honour, according to one of the detectives present, had a paper clip in his fingers that he appeared to be twirling vigorously as he looked at the big ex detective. But John Davidson had only one thing to say: 'I think I stated that YM2 was a friend of mine. Well I no longer consider him as such!'

He then stepped down. According to detectives inside the hearing room, you could have heard a pin drop. Not a word was said. The gathered detectives desperately tried to keep their faces hidden. John Davidson had just given the Royal Commission the answer they didn't want in front of a media throng.

The following day there were a number of media articles that reported the allegations against the detectives in detail with a few lines devoted to the officer's denials.

Later, on the day the detectives were getting their summonses to answer their charges on the Kareela Cat Burglar segment, I found the article by Kate McClymont in the *Sydney Morning Herald* on 1 July 1999. It is one of the most unfair stories I have seen in print.

Kate McClymont reported the charging of five senior police over the Kareela Cat Burglar allegations.

The police had already lost their jobs as a result of the accusations in 1997. This was an administrative procedure under Section 181 (d) of the Police Service Act where the NSW Police Commissioner alone could sack an officer because he had 'lost confidence' in them.

After detailing their police careers, McClymont then detailed some of the untested allegations made before the Wood Royal Commission by YM1, where he was not able to be cross-examined by any of the legal counsel for the five detectives. A point Ms McClymont forgot to mention. She repeated the untested allegations and said that several officers had rolled over.

These 'rollover' officers were never allowed to be cross-examined by the five accused officers at the WRC, ostensibly because it would 'delay' the proceedings. McClymont was reporting one side of the case, as no opportunity was given to the police officers accused of corruption to defend themselves.

McClymont did not know what was taking place behind closed doors at the Commission. One particular example was the interview conducted by McGinley and Stevens with a witness known as YM3. The interview was tape recorded and

YM3 continually denied any wrong doing until the tape was stopped midway through the interview.

When the interview was resumed, YM3 had a different story to tell. YM3 later admitted in court that he had been threatened by WRC investigators with prison if he didn't change his story. Did anyone in the Wood Royal Commission know about these tactics?

Ms McClymont would probably not have know that at the time, because YM3 and the other witnesses were not able to be cross-examined to see whether they were telling the truth or had been co-erced into making false statements.

The Wood Royal Commission into Corruption within the NSW Police was told that John Garvey, one of the five detectives involved in the arrest, and the other police then fabricated evidence against YM1 and perjured themselves in Court so that he could be convicted of 84 charges.

The same allegations were later raised in court proceedings involving the five detectives and that was found not to be the case.

Ms McClymont probably didn't know that the burglar had confessed or admitted to between 800-1000 burglaries in Victoria courtesy of a self promoting article in *Playboy* in December 1980, less than four years before to the Kareela incident.

Nor would she have probably been told by any of the Wood Royal Commission staff that the burglar had once nearly choked a five-day old baby in a hospital by placing his penis in the baby's mouth and ejaculating.

At the end of the committal hearing, the charges against all five of the former detectives were dismissed.

However, those five detectives never again wore the uniform of the NSW Police. Decades of loyal and courageous service to the people of New South Wales was forgotten. The detectives had to rebuild their lives as best as they could. Many of them suffered health problems and some still do. Personal relationships broke down as a result of the stress that they endured for many years over this disgraceful episode.

According to mutual friends of the detectives, their lives were irrevocably changed and they remain bitter and resentful of a system that hypocritically used the very tactics the detectives were accused of using with YM1, in order to pursue them in the name of the Wood Royal Commission. The difference being, that in spite of the comments of the Magistrate and the evidence of witnesses during the proceedings, no one has bothered to pursue the Royal Commission investigators. Why?

It is interesting to note certain comments made by Magistrate Barnett at the end of the committal hearing:

That the issues of credit and variance in testimony can be dealt with together and here the defence have had a field day.

Clearly in so far as character is concerned (YM1) is a despicable person.

The presiding Magistrate also observed that one of the WRC witnesses had previously lied to the Police Royal Commission and said:

One simply could not trust his evidence in all the circumstances. The defence have also raised related issues concerning the immunities and how the original statements of persons made to the Royal Commission investigators were adapted into formal statements, again these matters detract from the Prosecution case.

Perhaps most telling of the conduct of this matter came from the Crown Prosecutor's own observations. In a subsequent document to the DPP, he listed some of them:

The Court expressed serious reservations about the reliability of the evidence of each of the prosecution witnesses. Those reservations appeared to me to be well founded based on the evidence I saw given.

The Court gave an accurate assessment of the impact of the Defence witnesses called to rebut certain parts of the Prosecution case that were critical to the reliability of some of the prosecution evidence, particularly that given by …..[Former detective sergeant]

Without exception, those Defence witnesses presented very well, in some cases they presented as outstandingly credible witnesses. The Court recognised this in its assessment of their evidence.

In my view, the prosecution case was completely decimated by the end of the committal hearings.

One seldom sees a more comprehensive destruction of a prosecution case than occurred in these matters.

The conduct of the investigators at times material to the preparation of the witness's statements was open to serious criticism on the evidence given by each such witness.'

How did the Royal Commission investigators prepare the statements? Did these prepared statements match the verbal evidence given initially on taped recordings and then later transcribed into formal evidence?

There were a number of journalists present during the hearings and they duly reported the many concerns about the evidence given in the prosecution case. In this case, evidence emerged that investigators from the Royal Commission appear to have used threats to build prosecutions against five detectives it wanted to discredit. Why?

Was the primary reason for the pursuit of the five detectives not so much about what they were alleged to have done, but more for who they were and what they represented —'the old school cop'? It appears that whoever authorised or encouraged the investigators to use the tactics that they did, in order to gain prosecutions against the detectives, did so with little thought of the consequences, if any, down the track. The 'old school cop' was now an enemy of the state.

For Wood Royal Commission Investigator David McGinlay the controversy over his work with the commission was not over.

The matter of *Kim Hollingsworth -v- The Commissioner of Police* involved an action brought by a female former prostitute and stripper by the name of Kim Hollingsworth, who had been accepted into the NSW Police and was in training when it was discovered that she had not divulged details of her former occupation.

She was duly sacked when this came to light, and she sought reinstatement back into the Police Force via an Industrial Relations Court action. The matter was hard fought and lengthy and Ms Hollingsworth was initially successful in her legal action. That success was short-lived as the Commissioner of Police appealed the decision.

From examination of the *Hollingsworth –v- Commission of Police* NSW IRC 192 (22 December 1997) transcripts and *judgment*, the following story occurred during the proceedings of the Wood Royal Commission into Police Corruption.

Kim Hollingsworth was in part 'recruited' as a Wood Royal Commission informant through the efforts of former Commander Lola Scott, who was later sacked by Commissioner Ken Moroney but then reinstated and pensioned off. Ms Scott acted as a 'go between' for the Wood Royal Commission and Kim Hollingsworth in regard to evidence that she might have of alleged police corruption.

Eventually the Wood Royal Commission decided that Ms Hollingsworth needed to be relocated interstate for 'safety reasons' and she was moved to South Australia, where David McGinlay was a police officer.

During her time in Adelaide, Ms Hollingsworth, according to the IRC transcripts, went back to work as a prostitute due to financial problems she claims as a result of not being looked after by the Wood Royal Commission.

At the time Ms Hollingsworth worked as a prostitute in South Australia that practice was illegal and she obviously committed an offence. However, there is more to this story.

According to the IRC judgment:

The Commissioner also considered Ms Hollingsworth's return to prostitution after her dismissal, apparently a criminal offence in the State in question. The Commissioner came to no conclusion adverse to Ms Hollingsworth about this, apparently because of the involvement of the Royal Commission in those events.

The Commissioner observed:

I would have thought that if the Royal Commission required Ms Hollingsworth to be relocated interstate it would have made some arrangements to assist her in finding suitable employment. According to Senior Constable McGinlay, that did not happen in Ms Hollingsworth's case. Furthermore, Ms Hollingsworth work as a prostitute whilst she was relocated was with the knowledge of the Royal Commission investigators- Mr McGinlay and Ms EM Walker, a solicitor seconded to the Royal Commission, who was called as a witness in this part of the hearings by Mr Menzies-and the assistance of Mr McGinlay at least in the sense that he made inquiries and provided information to Ms Hollingsworth on which establishment she may work in safely and which establishments she should avoid.

Can this be true? We have an admission by a Commissioner of the IRC that he made no adverse conclusion to the offence Ms Hollingsworth committed in South Australia because of the involvement of the Wood Royal Commission. Was it a case that if the WRC had an interest in a matter then criminal offences could be committed and excused?

In many ways it is similar to the case of KX15 and the apparent breaking of the law in regard to the supply of hot heroin in Kings Cross. Who in the Wood Royal Commission knew about these activities and who approved it?

I find it intriguing that Investigator McGinlay made inquiries to ascertain which 'establishment' Ms Hollingsworth could work in with 'safety'. So just how did Investigator McGinlay make these inquiries? After all, prostitution was illegal in South Australia so I would not have thought that he would have contacted other serving South Australian Police Officers to get this information.

McGinlay is also alleged to have informed Ms Hollingsworth to avoid a particular Adelaide brothel owner because of the way he treated his 'girls' or his prostitutes.

Who knew about this within the upper echelons of the Wood Royal Commission?

Who authorised this utterly obscene and improper sequence of events that returned a woman back to prostitution after she had lost her position as a trainee police officer over that very occupation?

What makes a Royal Commission immune from not only scrutiny, but also prosecution?

4.

WHOSE WITNESS?
THE BODOR INQUIRY

The suburb of Cabramatta in Sydney's sprawling southwest has long been the first home for many new immigrants to Australia—from the early Italian settlers, to migrants from old Yugoslavia, Romania and finally to South East Asian migrants, particularly from Vietnam.

First-time visitors to the area are often enthralled by the Cabramatta CBD and its unique setting. The Asian-inspired shops and markets, the variety of South East Asian restaurants and the general atmosphere of the area makes visitors feel that they have arrived in Asia.

This unique setting came with some very unique problems for police and the NSW Government back in the 1990s. From the murder of John Newman, the local ALP Parliamentary Member in 1994 in what was Australia's first political assassination, to the gang wars of 1999-2000, the area became beset with major crime problems.

With the fallout from the Wood Royal Commission and the disastrous reign of Police Commissioner Peter Ryan, policing in Cabramatta collapsed and the suburb became Australia's heroin and homicide capital during the 1990s.

It was also through Cabramatta's crime problems that NSW policing came under the microscope yet again; just a few short years after Justice Wood handed down his final report of the Royal Commission into NSW Police Corruption. Ironically, corruption was not even on the radar in Cabramatta, but rather a total breakdown in law and order brought about by the failure of the rebuilt NSW Police Force to deal with gang and drug crime on a massive scale.

What I and many other police on the ground witnessed during the 1990s was a suburb brought to its knees by lawlessness and the scourge of heroin. In a sense, it was a suburb that had witnessed so much violence and human misery that it stopped caring for itself and became a hellhole for its many decent inhabitants.

Through the efforts of a few brave local residents, and with the support of frontline police at Cabramatta, the situation was turned around so much that it proved when local police and the community work together, rampant crime can be defeated.

What triggered this urban 'renewal' was the setting up of a NSW Parliamentary Inquiry into policing in the troubled suburb in 2000, the year of the Sydney Olympics.

It would also become one of the most controversial and highly charged inquiries in decades. Some observers say it was one of the most widely reported in the history of the NSW Parliament.

I made a number of appearances along with four other

Cabramatta police officers: Bob Francis, Greg Byrne, Vince Fusca and Chris Laird. Our appearance before the committee and the evidence we gave would become the subject of huge controversy and a media firestorm followed.

The Inquiry Committee was led by the highly respected NSW Legislative Council member, Helen Sham-Ho, a Hong Kong-born Australian.

Ms Sham-Ho displayed the leadership and courage that many current political leaders could do worse than emulate. She was a quietly spoken but determined character, and left a lasting impression on the street cops and the community witnesses that attended her hearings.

One of the witnesses that appeared before her on 10 May 2001 used the assumed name of 'James Ross' to protect his identity. This courageous young man, who had led a sad and troubled life, decided to come forward and tell the inquiry and the New South Wales Police what he knew about drugs, gangs and crimes in Cabramatta. He was a rare bird. His evidence was held in camera (away from media and in front of the committee members only) for a variety of reasons, many of which were to protect his identity and personal security.

'James' told the inquiry about gangs, weapons and drugs in school playgrounds and other sites across Cabramatta. He outlined the massive problems associated with the area and gave first-hand experience of drug dealing and the associated violence that goes with it. He also gave evidence about drugs and violence in one of the local high schools that also caused considerable debate within the community and the government.

Following his in camera appearance before the Inquiry, an approach was made by the area's Police Commander, Clive

Small, to debrief James on his knowledge of the Asian gang, drug and crime problems in the area.

A police inquiry was conducted under the auspices of Commander Clive Small and Acting Inspector Sergeant Matt Appleton and James was interviewed at length. The findings of their investigation were set out in a document that became known as the 'James Report'. Its legacy and the huge controversy that surrounds this report still linger today.

The James Report, its contents, the way James was investigated and the way the report was distributed, was the subject of written complaints made by myself, Frank Reitano and Doctor Richard Basham to Peter Ryan's successor, Commissioner Ken Maroney.

The formal written complaint raised the following concerns:

1. The apparent leaking of the James Report to certain sections of the media, including Chris Masters and Mike Carlton

2. The substance of the report

3. James's treatment by Clive Small and Matt Appleton

4. The fact that involved Police Officers were not allowed to view the report.

Faced with a written complaint, these issues were then examined at the behest of the NSW Police Force in an inquiry under the direction of Peter Bodor QC: The Bodor Inquiry.

HOW WAS THE JAMES REPORT COMPILED?

One of the most contentious aspects that Peter Bodor QC was asked to look into was the way the content of the James Report was compiled.

The James Report was said to debunk James's accounts of drug dealing. This was seized upon by Police Commissioner Peter Ryan to justify a position he had publicly taken on the level of crime in Cabramatta. Ryan attempted to portray the level of crime and the volume of drugs being dealt there as under control, and played down the seriousness of the situation. Regardless of the implications of the James Report, the situation on the ground in Cabramatta never changed. Ryan was clearly isolated from his advisors in Cabramatta, a situation that inevitably led to his downfall.

Dr Richard Basham, Detective Sergeant Frank Reitano and myself have gone on record as saying that the motives behind the investigation into James's allegations were intentionally eschewed to play down the real crisis that was taking place on the streets of Cabramatta. Subsequently, James' integrity as a reliable informant was severely questioned, and 27 of the 30 allegations he had made in the Inquiry were dismissed.

Just before the James Report was completed, Clive Small was seconded to the Premier's Department and finalisation of the report was inherited by the acting Region Commander, Superintendent Les Wales.

Wales took over a temporary role as Region Commander and oversaw the final draft of the James Report. Despite requesting Matt Appleton to carry out further checks and enquiries, Wales ultimately signed off on the report.

In the transcripts of the interviews with Peter Bodor QC, Wales indicates that he was eventually happy with the final report, signed off on it and produced it to the then Deputy Commissioner Dave Madden.

However, Peter Bodor QC, when interviewing Les Wales,

asked him a few very simple but extraordinary questions:

> *Peter Bodor QC: For example and I'm just plucking one out of the air during the course of the drive around with James, he identified a number of vehicles as being associated with certain people and criminal activities?*
>
> *Les Wales: Yes.*
>
> *Peter Bodor QC: Now, it doesn't appear, for example, that those registration numbers have been checked out?*
>
> *Les Wales: I don't know about that. I don't remember that.*
>
> *Peter Bodor QC: Sorry?*
>
> *Les Wales: I don't remember that.*
>
> *Peter Bodor QC: Well, when you say you don't remember that, do you mean you have no memory one way or the other or your memory is different?*
>
> *Les Wales: If that's in the James Report, if that is, and I don't know, I don't remember that. I don't know the report inside out. It's been a while now.*
>
> *Peter Bodor QC: I understand that, but would it strike you as being a deficiency in an investigation, where a car registration number is linked to an individual or a criminal activity, not to follow through the car registration?*
>
> *Les Wales: If in fact that is the case, I would agree with that. If that is the case, I would agree with that.*

Cars identified to criminals and their associates did not apparently warrant simple rego checks and perhaps police intelligence reports to see what and who they were connected to? The most basic of all investigative tools is usually to find the names, addresses and vehicles belonging to suspects and then expand that search to include their associates. In a major investigation like the James Report, such an omission is almost unbelievable.

In 2002 after the James Report had been written, Chris Masters and the ABC released a television program called *Jonestown*, which covered issues in Cabramatta. While this was going out to the nation via the public television broadcaster, James himself contacted Richard Basham, Frank Reitano and others and complained about the way he had been handled by Clive Small and Matt Appleton during the investigation of his claims about Cabramatta.

After his brave appearance at the Parliamentary Inquiry, Richard Basham, myself, Frank Reitano and other police officers, had convinced James that he should co-operate with the police and help us to gather real intelligence about who was doing what on the ground in Cabramatta. Clive Small was given the task of leading this investigation.

Even though James expressed reservations about Clive Small, Richard, Frank and I convinced James to assist Clive Small to try to expose some of the major leaders and stem the tide of crime in the area.

In retrospect, this was one of the biggest mistakes we could have made.

As part of the arrangement under which James agreed to assist Clive Small and Matt Appleton, certain safeguards were put in place to protect James. It was agreed that copies of all the taped recorded interviews with James were to be handed to Richard Basham for safekeeping. That was agreed to by Clive Small as it was a reasonable and common police practice to give copies of tapes of interviews to witnesses. The reason was also that in the event that something controversial was said or put to James, then James had a later copy to see exactly what had been said. This was primarily to protect James' own rights.

However, for a reason that remains unknown, these tapes were never supplied to James.

Frank Reitano was initially selected by Clive Small to conduct the de-briefing of James. This made sense as Reitano was born and raised in Cabramatta. Frank was also an extremely competent detective who had considerable knowledge of Asian crime and Asian offenders.

James had grown up in a troubled environment in Cabramatta, and although he was Caucasian Australian, he had little connection with the traditional Australian way of life. He was, without appearing racist, semi-Asian. He had grown to respect the Asians, his language in many instances imitated the fast staccato-like delivery of Asian youths and he acted like them physically, for example squatting while socializing as Asian youths are prone to do. He related to the Asian culture more than he did the traditional Australian culture.

Asian crime investigation is an art form. There are many nuances involved with the identification of Asian offenders, particularly South East Asian offenders. The names can be confusing. The community can mix the first with the second traditional names, and has a prolific use of limited 'family names', such as Tran, Nguyen, Huynh, etc. The names quite often will supply little information to help in readily identifying people. Add to that a blending of English-style first names with traditional Vietnamese surnames, and it becomes almost impossible at times to separate dozens of suspects with exactly the same names. The only way to accurately do this was to identify them using prints or photos.

Frank Reitano was well aware of this problem.

So, as the good Asian crime investigator he was, Frank Reitano planned to use photographs to assist with identifying the offenders that James was providing information on. But suddenly it was not Frank Reitano who led the investigation. Matt Appleton took over as chief debriefer. Matt Appleton was an experienced police officer, but not in the crucial area of Asian crime, a point later highlighted by Peter Bodor QC in his final report.

It was pointless interviewing James the same way as you would a kid from Blacktown, Redfern, Bondi or Manly. You would never get the responses you hoped for. And this is exactly what Matt Appleton got in his debriefing of James. Despite Frank Reitano repeatedly telling him to use photos when James mentioned Asian offenders, Matt Appleton did not use this technique.

It didn't take long for James to also lose confidence in Matt Appleton.

When the interviews were completed, the transcripts were expected to be forwarded by Matt Appleton to Frank Reitano to assist in identifying matters that would have to be referred to an Asian Task Force for follow up. Neither the transcripts nor the tapes were given to Frank Reitano as per the initial agreement. As well, astoundingly, no follow up on the potentially critical allegations and information James gave in these interviews appear to have been done. And James himself seems to have been left entirely unprotected. Hardly an incentive for good community and police relations.

On 6 June 2002, lawyer Paul Kenny made contact with James. James provided him with a statutory declaration that for the first time told his side of the story, the contents of which are self-explanatory:

> I...met with Mr Small and Detective Matthew Appleton and Frank Reitano at a secret location. My [grand]mother was there as well. As far as I was aware the purpose of that meeting was for the police to clarify what I said at the Inquiry and on those shows. Clive Small did all the talking...at first he promised, as best as I can remember, for me to have immunity from prosecution, that we would be protected by the police and be relocated, that we would have financial support, and that we would be taken care of. I felt very scared about all of this. I had never done anything like this before and things had already happened to me because I came forwarded [sic] and I had been threatened by people in Cabramatta...
>
> Detective Appleton conducted a number of interviews with me, and, right from the start it was obvious to me that he had no knowledge of criminal activity in Cabramatta or of Asian crime in general. He didn't seem to understand what I was talking about at all half the time but Frank Reitano and Richard Basham knew all about the people and things I was talking about and they had to explain things to Detective Appleton.
>
> As far as I was concerned Frank Reitano and/or Richard Basham were to be present when I was being interviewed and after the first few interviews Frank and Richard did not come to the interviews. I asked Detective Appleton why

they were not present and he told me that Frank Reitano had been put on other duties and that Richard Basham did not want anything to do with it anymore or he could not get hold of Richard, or words to that effect.

At some stage during the interviews with Detective Appleton he asked me if I wanted to make a complaint against any Police. I told him about some things in the past. At no stage during the interviews with Detective Appleton did he ever suggest that I was lying about things or that I was making things up but he did say that there was [sic] too many inconsistencies. I didn't know what he was talking about...

When the interviews and the Police Investigation were finished Detective Appleton contacted me and asked me to come to Sydney to sign a piece of paper. He didn't tell me what the piece of paper was but he told me he would have a solicitor there for me and that they would move us to a new house at a different location. I went to Sydney to Police Headquarters and Detective Appleton met me and my [grand]mother and father downstairs. We went upstairs to a room and he spoke to me in complicated terms about a paper. Then he went outside and brought in another man to witness the paper. There was no lawyer there as he had promised. He said the lawyer wasn't there yet but he would get him to have a look at the papers later. I said I wanted a lawyer there but a lawyer never arrived. Detective Appleton told me to read the paper over and sign it. I could not understand what the paper was about and I gave it to my [grand]mother to read but she couldn't read it because she didn't have her glasses. Detective Appleton said 'once you sign this paper we can get the ball rolling and move you'. I signed the paper and said 'What's this all about' and he said 'This is so you can't sue us if you try and say that we didn't look after you' or words to that effect. I didn't know what he was talking about and then he asked if I wanted a copy of the paper and I said 'Yes'. He didn't give me a copy then but said it would be forwarded to me. Detective Appleton also asked if I wanted copies of the tapes of the interviews I did with him and I said 'Yes'. He said that he would forward copies of the tapes to me but I have not received them yet. He also asked about Richard Basham and Frank Reitano and if I wanted them to have a copy of the paper and copies of the tapes and I said 'Yes'. Then Detective Appleton said words to the effect of that I would not want these tapes and the paper being shown to the media and I told him to only send a copy to me. I asked him about our move and he said 'Leave it all to me'. After I and my [grand]mother signed the paper Detective Appleton told us that Clive Small had said to give us some money for our new start and he gave me $500 for furniture and $300 for fares and then we left.

Since that time we have not been moved or protected in any way. I want Detective Appleton to give me a copy of the paper I signed and I want copies of the taped interviews I did with him. I want those things to be forwarded to my new solicitor, Paul Kenny.

I have a number of Asian friends who were prepared to assist the Police with information but because of what has happened to me being abandoned by the Police they are not prepared to assist at this stage.

I am now in grave fear for my own personal safety and for

my family and I request that the Parliamentary Committee or some other section of the government do something to help us. Under no circumstances whatsoever do I want anything further to do with Detective Appleton or Clive Small and I do not wish to have any form of communication with any member of the New South Wales Police Force unless I am in the company of my solicitor, or any legal representative or any other person appointed by him.

The failures by the police force to fulfill its obligations to James have never been investigated.

HOW DID THE REPORT END UP IN THE MEDIA BEFORE THE POLICE EXECUTIVE?

Peter Bodor QC was asked to conduct an inquiry on the James Report on the following three points:

1.   Is there any evidence that any individual or otherwise, has brought any inappropriate influence or pressure on the investigation into allegations made by the person 'James';
2.   Is there any evidence that the investigation is flawed?
3.   Should the report on the allegations by 'James' be released on general or limited basis?

Critically, one aspect of the initial complaint, namely the way in which the James Report had been circulated to members of the media prior to it being submitted to the police executive, was not referred to Bodor to examine. This was the one crucial question missing from the terms of reference outlined to

Peter Bodor QC in the letter from Michael Holmes, General Manager Court and Legal Services, dated 21 March 2003. It was, inexplicably, to my mind, not included in the letter to Peter Bodor QC.

Why it never was still remains a source of concern to me and other police involved in the James saga. It was I believe the easiest to prove, given that two television programs had referred to material in the confidential report and Chris Masters had declared in his emails to Richard Basham that he had seen the report.

Even though Commissioner Ryan criticized the role the media played in the Cabramatta debacle, the role of certain sections of the media in the distribution and reporting on the James Report dramatically highlights the often unethical relationships that can develop between journalists, senior politicians and police.

In the transcripts of the Bodor Inquiry, Les Wales relates to Peter Bodor QC that even before he had a chance to complete the final report on James's allegations, he had a phone call from radio 2UE disc jockey Mike Carlton. Carlton wanted to interview Wales on air in relation to the yet to be completed James Report. How is it that Mike Carlton knew that the James Report was being prepared? And why did he want to interview the police officer tasked with its completion prior to it being finished?

Peter Bodor asked Les Wales about this in his examination:

Les Wales: Yes, I asked Clive issues—I did speak to Clive about, 'where's this, what's this mean?' My exact memory of that issue and those conversations I don't remember, but there was conversation in the early part as to what it was, where it was. I was unaware, not across some of the, I guess media issues, the political issues, of the day in relation to it per se. I was asked by Mike Carlton to in fact speak to him on air, which I refused to do, obviously because it wasn't complete, it wasn't my role to do and I refused to do it, but I had to in fact speak to Clive early in the piece to clarify issues about the document.

Notwithstanding that Wales didn't agree to go on air with him, Mike Carlton said his sources were 'experienced detectives', who knew about a 'tissue of fantasy' from James concerning his allegations about Cabramatta. This article appeared in the *Sydney Morning Herald* on 11 May 2002:

I have numbered the many errors contained in Carlton's article with the real facts in a paragraph below the story.

Headline: Let's have the facts about Cabramatta

When our crime busting Police Minister Michael Costa....... He will release what has become known around the traps as the James Report. (1) James you may recall was an 18 year old from Cabramatta (2) whose lurid account of gangs, guns and drugs in school playgrounds terrified the entire city last year when the media got hold of him......
(3) He was a gang member himself.......Kids were killing each other for the thrill of it...(4). There were drug gangs recruiting in all of the schools...... (5) The resulting panic led to the setting up of a State Parliamentary committee investigating policing in Cabramatta and (6) eventually to the downfall of the then Police Minister Paul Whelan and

the Commissioner Peter Ryan....

(7) Sad to reveal then that James's story was a tissue of fantasy.... (8). Experienced Detectives have investigated his allegations found to be either entirely untrue or at best wildly exaggerated... (9) The kid had never been a gang member...... (10) Nor had he attended the strife torn Cabramatta High School... (11)...I am told it's all there in the James report..... The Parliament and public have a right to see it. (12) Unfilleted...

Now for the facts.

1. James was 16 years old, a minor, he was not 18.

2. His account of gangs, guns and drugs in school playgrounds was supported by evidence given to the Parliamentary Inquiry by Officers A, B, C and D under oath and reported by David Penberthy in the *Daily Telegraph* on 1 May 2001. Officer A confirmed a 'number of intelligence reports saying there is current activity in the schools to recruit kids to different gangs'. Asked if Cabramatta High School was one of those, Officer A replied 'Yes'. In addition to this evidence, there are police records of a female student from Cabramatta High School arrested with her mother for a large commercial supply of heroin in 1999.

3. James never claimed to be a gang member. He hung around with gang members, including those from the 5T, but he was not Asian and therefore ineligible to join. He was an associate, in much the same way as 'wise guys' or associates are with the US mafia, where to join you must be Italian born or be of Italian descent.

4. Again evidence under oath by Cabramatta officers, with

police intelligence files, supported his evidence.

5. The Cabramatta Inquiry commenced in the year 2000. I gave my first evidence in November 2000, some seven months before James went before the Committee and eight months before he went on *60 Minutes*. The Cabramatta Inquiry was actually set up after repeated complaints by local community members with the support of Cabramatta street cops. It had absolutely nothing to do with James's evidence. Carlton's time frame is out by about 230 days, nearly a year.

6. If James could not and did not help set up the Cabramatta Inquiry, then how did that lead to the downfall of Paul Whelan and Peter Ryan?

7. Tissue of fantasy? Not according to Peter Bodor QC in his final report to the NSW Police Commissioner.

8. 'Experienced' detectives working on the case—there was Matt Appleton, Clive Small and Frank Reitano. Frank Reitano is on record as saying he believed James. So that just leaves Clive Small and Matt Appleton as the 'experienced' detectives. Matt Appleton had little experience in investigating Asian organized crime. The inquiry by Peter Bodor QC was scathing of the 'experienced detectives' that wrote the James Report. So which one of the two 'experienced detectives' divulged 'highly confidential' material to Mike Carlton while the ink was still drying on the report and before it had even reached the Deputy Police Commissioner?

9. When and where did James claim to have been a gang member?

10. James never said in any forum, that he went to

Cabramatta High School. He went to Canley Vale High School.

11. Isn't it an offence to divulge police records and confidential crime reports to unauthorized persons? Was Mike Carlton an authorized person?

12. 'Unfilleted', I don't know.

There were only three detectives who had knowledge of James' allegations to begin with and only two knew of the findings—Clive Small and Matt Appleton.

In August 2002, Mike Carlton gave evidence to Parliament in the Cabramatta Inquiry. He named Peter Ryan as one of his sources at dinner parties and Clive Small as another at lunchtime in a pub somewhere in Sydney.

Shortly after the James Report was submitted to Police Headquarters in May 2002, an ABC *Four Corners* program called *Jonestown* went to air. Journalist Chris Masters covered James' allegations about drugs and violence in Cabramatta and focused on the Sydney personality and radio broadcaster Alan Jones, particularly in relation to Alan Jones' many interviews and opinions on crime in Cabramatta.

In that TV program, Masters accuses Richard Basham of 'helping hawk the boy around the media'. He then discloses, on national television, material from the highly confidential James Report.

Chris Masters says on the program:

> *Following an extensive review, police have since discovered the attack James described on the shop did not occur. James has now admitted he did not belong to a gang or witness the sale of guns.*

How is it that Chris Masters was able to canvass in the course of his exposé on Alan Jones material that was contained within a confidential internal police investigation into the matters that James had raised before the Parliamentary Inquiry?

In emails sent by Chris Masters to Richard Basham, which he gave to Peter Bodor QC, Masters clearly and unequivocally admits that he has or has seen the 'Review' of the James Report, as does John Lyons [a Channel 9 journalist] later on. Frank Reitano, Richard Basham and I did not have the chance to go over the report before it was finalized.

An email from Chris Masters to Richard Basham on 4 May 2002 said:

> *The promised email I discover has bounced back so I am resubmitting. The questions I wanted to put to you were covered in our phone call. Since we spoke I have seen the review of the 'James' report which does reject the great majority of the assertions, ie that he belonged to a gang and witnesses the sale of firearms as alleged etc. I know we did speak about this. If you believe there is a particular reason to disbelieve the police review you might let me know.*

To this day, the James Report has never been released for public scrutiny.

Consequently neither myself, nor the other serving police who gave evidence at the Cabramatta Inquiry, have ever seen it.

In the *Jonestown* TV program, Chris Masters followed the same line that Commissioner Ryan had and downplayed the amount of crime in Cabramatta. He complained that Alan Jones did not respond to complaints from John Steinmetz from

Cabramatta High School. John Steinmetz was quoted on the *Four Corners* program [responding to a quote from Alan Jones which said that the schools had their heads in the sand and had no idea of what was happening in their community] and said:

> *If these things were happening and we didn't know about them, and we had our head in the sand, as Mr. Jones alludes, ok, that'd be bad enough. When it's not true, then it's so soul destroying.*

I have no doubt that the teachers at Cabramatta High School are as much on the ball as they possibly can be, but even they can't know everything that goes on in the school yard. However, either John Steinmetz was not at Cabramatta High School on 22 November 1999 or he forgot about yet another 'incident'. This incident occurred during the lead up to the all out gang war in Cabramatta in 1999, which extended into 2000. This was the sort of incident that led to the formulation of the Cook Report on violence in Cabramatta.

> *NSW Police COPS Event No. 16129201- 22 November 1999.*
>
> *Gidgee Street Cabramatta, 40 Students Brawling—This event indicates that a non student attended Cabramatta High School during a lunchtime break and commenced to hand out weapons to students. The weapons included machetes and steel bars. As a result of the ensuing brawl an offender was charged with Affray and Malicious Wounding.*

This was just one of a number of incidents, not necessarily on the grounds of Cabramatta High School, but either nearby or involving students from local high schools.

The above incident was fairly well known and had serious implications for everybody in the community—police, education, health and courts. It is not the sort of incident one would forget in 12 months or so.

I remain curious as to why John Steinmetz was interviewed on the *Jonestown* program instead of the Deputy Principal of Cabramatta High School, who was the teacher reported as handling the incident I referred to in my parliamentary evidence He was the source that had reported the matter to police.

Included in the *Jonestown* program was Dr David Dixon from the Law Faculty at the University of New South Wales, who also appeared on Mike Carlton's radio program with similar comments. Dr Dixon is quoted saying:

> *I don't think that exaggerating fears about crime and exaggerating the potential of the police to deal with crime problems is doing anything to make the streets safer at all.*

Dixon is entitled to his opinion, no doubt based on what he refers to as empirical evidence. The reality is that many people have a fear of crime in certain parts of this city and it is not exaggerated and the potential for police to deal with crime problems I would suggest is far greater than a criminologist's potential to solve crime. You only have to look at the police inspired zero tolerance strategy from New York's NYPD to see that police are the difference most times in crime control.

A THOROUGH INVESTIGATION?

The James Report was submitted to the Deputy Commissioner of Police as having been a 'thorough investigation' of the allegations raised by James.

How thorough was it? Peter Bodor QC managed to see through the personal attacks, misinformation and unsupported allegations that were made during the witnesses' interviews with Clive Small.

However, the conclusion by Peter Bodor QC raised more questions than it solved. It highlights areas that required further investigation and points out 'matters alerting suspicion'. His final remarks read as follows:

> *I am clearly aware that highly committed, intelligent and professional witnesses on oath before GPSC3 and elsewhere have exposed or related their knowledge and beliefs regarding the history of this matter to whoever was, or is, prepared to listen. Some have willingly jeopardized their careers, reputations and legal actions by expressing the views that they have.*
>
> *There is a welter of allegations, innuendo and suspicion that Clive Small for his own purposes (and perhaps that of others) exerted improper control over the investigation of James's allegations and the James Report.*
>
> *That Clive Small alone, or with/for others had the capacity to influence the outcome of the James Investigation and Report is obvious. However, it is glib to assume that Clive Small corrupted the James Investigation because a particular result was not achieved by those who wanted to see a particular*

Policing/Political corner turned in Cabramatta.

I am of the view that there is no sustainable evidence that would answer Q1 in the affirmative when one attempts to 'connect the dots', there is no clear picture, even on the balance of probabilities that Small or anyone else acted improperly.

There is, nonetheless, ample room for suspicion, that the investigation and the report thereafter were contrived, not to reflect the full facts.

Matters alerting suspicion can be best derived from an examination of the Chronological Summary (annexure 2) and include:

The appointment of Appleton who had little or no knowledge of the historical background to Cabramatta policing and who was considered an outsider

That Small never read the James debriefing and was totally reliant only on Appleton's account of the information James provided to identify issues (Small 26.5.03.) a 'curiously inexact, opaque process of identifying issues and detail'.

Progress drafts of the James Report being transmitted to Small's private email address (Small 26.5.03. T32 (Vol 8, Tabs 17, 21, 28), suggesting a distinct approach to the preparation of the James Report from investigation procedures.

Absence of any recorded trail of conversations or investigative strategies between Small and Appleton.

Appleton kept inquiry "pretty close to his chest" and reported directly to Small and did not really keep Hanson updated with what was going on (Appleton 12.5.03. T-19) or apparently anyone else.

Appleton's lack of record keeping, disclosing the methodology and investigations undertaken, contradicting Small's assertion that part of his brief to Appleton was to record 'everything' in writing regarding the investigation (Small 26.5.03. T.31)

The 'part time' nature of the investigation.

Appleton conducting the investigation alone, given its scope and sensitivity.

The contradictory evidence between Small and Appleton regarding Reitano's role. Small asserting Reitano was clearly intended as an investigator and that Reitano should be part of the investigation at every point, 'so the other side would have trouble criticizing the investigation'.(Small 23.5.03. T1-p 65-66 with Small having no doubt that Appleton knew Reitano would be working alongside (Small 26.5.03.T 27-29, 36), whereas Appleton thought of Reitano merely as a support person for James(later 'modified' in interview) and not an investigator (Appleton 12.5.03. T.14, 16, 30). Later 'diluted'

That Appleton was aware after 'discussions' that there were Serious allegations of Impropriety against him in 2001(IA File) and that Small as Commander of Greater Hume Region and in 'close liaison' over the James investigation, could reasonably be assumed to have some knowledge of the existence of the allegations against Appleton.

The 'matters alerting suspicion' that Peter Bodor QC listed were major concerns. They should have been acted upon by the Police Integrity Commission.

Also, if Carlton was aware of what Bodor had found, he may

have reconsidered his characterization of those who debriefed James as 'experienced' detectives.

One particular point in Bodor's comments amazes me. That is that Clive Small and Matt Appleton were corresponding on the progress and direction of the James investigation via private emails and not using the police computer system. Why would they have done that? The police email system is always used in matters like this. It is an accountable, corruption resistant means of monitoring information being shared across the Police computer network.

Those emails would have shown exactly what was going on between Clive Small and Matt Appleton at a time when Frank Reitano made constant enquiries about being included in the investigation process and the final report. Had those emails been available, many of the allegations made by Reitano, Basham and myself could have been readily and succinctly answered one way or the other.

More importantly, Peter Bodor QC may have been able to investigate serious questions about the James Report that still remain unanswered. It would have also shown how these two 'experienced' detectives came to the final conclusion that James's story was a 'tissue of lies'.

Many at the time questioned that emails on private providers can be tracked, so these emails could have been traced and read, but Peter Bodor QC did not have the power to go further than ask for Small's co-operation with these private emails. I am unaware if Peter Bodor QC was ever able to view the contents of Clive Small's private email exchanges with Matt Appleton over the James Report.

So with no power to summons witnesses, seize documents,

or conduct lawful searches say of internet emails, Peter Bodor QC could do nothing other than accept Clive Small's version of the reasons for this unprecedented email usage and what was contained in those emails. It is little wonder that Peter Bodor QC could never 'join the dots'.

Peter Bodor QC did his best under difficult and convoluted circumstances. He concluded by saying that he accepted that:

> ...James was at all times doing his best with police and his attempts to assist must be respected and commended with the sincerest gratitude. His courage in coming forward was very impressive.
>
> I (Bodor QC) consider that a more supportive and thorough investigation may well have yielded more specific and more valuable information.

Nowhere in Peter Bodor QC's final remarks on James and the James Report, did he say that James's allegations were a 'tissue of lies'. In fact, Peter Bodor QC says that a 'more supportive and thorough investigation may well have yielded more specific and valuable information.'

The final report that was delivered to Commissioner Moroney was not the anticipated in-depth inquiry with investigative powers. How did that happen? Many people are still asking the same question. In the fullness of time, the Bodor Inquiry Report was submitted to parliament in April 2004 and no action was taken, against anyone.

Where are the people who could answer these questions?

Clive Small was, at the time of the Bodor Inquiry, an adviser to the Premier's Department on Community Safety. He would later be appointed Director of Investigations at the Independent Commission Against Corruption, then headed by Irene Moss.

Matt Appleton is now an Acting Superintendent of Police.

Frank Reitano is still a Sergeant and working as a Prosecutor at a Sydney suburban local court.

Dr Richard Basham retired at age 60 from the University of Sydney and left Australia, returning to his home in America's south. After living in Australia for 30 years, he had grown tired of what he described as the 'perversion of the noble occupation of investigative journalism'.

'James' lives somewhere in NSW, disillusioned and trying to turn his life around.

5.

OFF THE RECORD

No sooner had the ink dried on the Bodor Inquiry report, the issues were again raised and dissected in the public forum—on the ABC and in the newspapers.

Despite the seriousness of the issues raised in the Bodor Inquiry, several journalists became fixated with me, other police colleagues and media personalities. Their reporting raises several questions about influence, information sources, and the ability of police officers to carry out their duties in an atmosphere of trust and accountability.

This early example alerted me to what was to become somewhat of a pattern. In the *Sydney Morning Herald* in 2004 journalist Mike Carlton wrote:

> *I was surprised to read, though, that Priest claimed 'he had material which could destroy Carlton and that the Premier had to go because he lied about Ryan being a good Commissioner*

and that he also had dirt on the Premier' (sic).

I went through all of the testimonies in the Bodor Inquiry to find where he had sourced this claim. It was definitely not in the hundred or so pages of my interview to the Inquiry. So I went through Frank Reitano's testimony, Richard Basham's and so on until I found it, almost word for word. Mike Carlton was quoting from an interview conducted by Peter Bodor QC with Clive Small, where Clive Small claimed I had said this. I never said this and Clive Small appears to be the only living person with a recollection of this supposed conversation.

Instead of focussing on the 'matters alerting suspicion' that Peter Bodor QC had raised, which asked several serious questions about the conduct of the James investigation and the compilation of the James Report (see previous chapter for these), the focus of this *Herald* article was Clive Small's testimony about a supposed 'dirt file' on the Premier that I was supposed to have. *It was not true and I never said it.*

That hearsay evidence is based on supposition and not fact.

Two years after the Bodor Inquiry into the James Report was released, Chris Masters went to print with his book called *Jonestown*, in which he charted the life and career of radio personality Alan Jones. My involvement with Alan Jones represents a small component of that story. Nevertheless, I featured quite extensively in that book.

Masters revisited the Bodor Inquiry in that book. But I wonder if his research included trawling through the hundreds of pages of transcripts of the Bodor Inquiry as I have done. I subsequently sued Masters and his publisher Allan and Unwin over Masters' book. They settled with me out of court.

The 2006 *Four Corners* program called *Jonestown* was I believe, the precursor to Masters' book of the same name.

Masters rang me while he was making the *Jonestown* program and said he wanted to interview me. I think he felt that I was obliged to talk to him because I had criticised the Wood Royal Commission (see chapter 1). I spoke to him for some minutes before I hung up on him. In those brief few minutes of conversation, I quickly came to the conclusion that I had said things in the media that had obviously irked him and he wanted to take issue with me on television. Ordinarily, I probably would have agreed, but something about Masters during that very brief conversation warned me not to.

I did agree to meet with Chris Masters 'off the record' at a coffee shop near St James railway station in central Sydney. I took a close friend with me, former drug squad colleague and now criminal lawyer, Paul Kenny.

The meeting, it would be fair to say, was not easy and I reaffirmed my refusal to take part in Chris' television program, which he said was focussed on Alan Jones.

We parted soon after and Masters duly described me as a 'turbulent detective' on the program. It is important to remember that the meeting with Masters was strictly 'off the record'. But Chris Masters broke that code of ethics and repeated many of our conversations in the public arena.

During the conversation at the coffee shop I supposedly referred to Peter Ryan as a liar. My recollection of that conversation was that I thought Ryan had lied about the seriousness of crime in Cabramatta and in particular about the motives of myself and the so-called 'Cabramatta 4', in criticising the lack of police focus on gangs in the area (see *To Protect and To Serve* and Chapter 4 in this book). There was a remark attributed to Ryan that the police rebellion at Cabramatta came as a result of us being 'shifted out of our cosy little positions at Cabramatta Police Station'. What Ryan said was clearly wrong and I thought it was a lie.

In 2002 Sue Williams wrote a book on the former Commissioner Peter Ryan, *The Peter Ryan Story*. Chris Masters reviewed that book for the *Sydney Morning Herald* 10 August 2002 and took the opportunity to talk about Internal Affairs 'problems' with me and also that I called Ryan a liar. Whether I did or didn't and whether it was in the context that Masters wrote is irrelevant. What was said between Masters and I was 'off the record' and to repeat a selected word or words in a review of the subject I had spoken about was poor form. In my view it breached a duty of confidence that Masters had encouraged in me.

Masters and I shared a mutual friend, former undercover detective, Michael Drury. Mick has been a close friend of mine for nearly 25 years, going back to our Drug Squad days in the 1980s. Masters had known Drury for a similar period, probably since Mick survived his near fatal assassination at the hands of Christopher Flannery in 1984.

Drury had known for some time about the bad relationship between Masters and I and felt that some common ground should be reached in order for Masters to accurately report facts and sequences of events in his forthcoming book of the TV program, *Jonestown*. I agreed and met Masters again, this time at a cafe near Central Station on 1 May 2005 at 10.12am. I was running late as I recall.

We sat down, ordered coffees and began to chat. I came away

from that conversation with the impression that Chris throught Alan Jones suspected there was a dirt file on him within the Police Force, and he wanted to find it. No dirt file ever existed on Alan Jones. It was an invention.

In his evidence before Bodor QC, Clive Small had also attributed to me knowledge of a 'dirt file' on the Premier of NSW. This had found its way into the article by Mike Carlton in a quote attributed to me.

I recall cautioning Chris Masters about believing anything that certain people said, especially where it related to Alan Jones, Richard Basham, Frank Reitano and myself. I tried to explain, in simple terms, the story of Cabramatta, the crime and the many internal police inquiries. I actually thought he understood.

I told him that Clive Small had commenced an action in the Industrial Relations Court against the NSW Police Force, after Commissioner Ken Maroney had refused to renew his contract.

We spoke about a range of topics, about me in particular, and some of the correspondence I had with Police Internal Affairs over the years that was a source of great interest to Masters.

I explained to him that Internal Affairs complaints are part and parcel of street policing and the life of a policeman. The more arrests you make, the more complaints you are likely to attract. I have made more arrests than most detectives—that is not a boast. There are a number of former senior police that were bosses of mine at various locations that can and do attest to that—the Drug Squad, the NCA, Liverpool and Green Valley, Redfern, City Central.

They are living, breathing, identifiable human beings—Former

Assistant Commissioner Dennis Gilligan, Former Assistant Commissioner Geoff Schuberg, Superintendent Don Graham, Former Detective Chief Inspector Tony Waters, former Detective Chief Inspector Brett Cooper, I could go on.

Chris Masters expressed his attitude that the whole of the police force needed to be turned over and that there was no need for the 'old cops' of yesteryear in an era we now face of wanton and uncontrolled violence. He agreed there was a need for some of these experienced and well-honed detective skills, but that was tempered by allegations of corruption that he believed 'seemingly' only afflicted the 'old guard'. Old guard equalled corruption in his eyes.

From 2004 until 2005, Masters and I swapped emails with each other over various policing topics. I have kept all of them. One of those email exchanges involved a Masters quote in an interview where he described police in the 1980s as 'having so spectacularly let us (the community) down'.

I reminded him via email of the many, many NSW Police Officers who had died in the line of duty in the 1980s protecting people that they had never met, but had sworn an oath to protect. Such courageous officers like Constable Alan McQueen, gunned down in Hyde Park in broad daylight, of Constable Paul Quinn from Bathurst, who was gunned down on a deserted country road and many, many more. They all left behind families and grieving relatives that at least had the comfort of knowing they died bravely for the community they had sworn an oath to protect.

Meanwhile, at the coffee shop, Chris told me that his son had been assaulted somewhere north of the city and was now alarmed at being assaulted again. This a typical young male victim in Sydney and I sympathise with him. It is an alarming problem, worse than I have seen in the past three decades. It's a situation that calls for a recognition of a mixed police force, one that uses the experience of the older policemen with the youth and vigour of the new recruits.

Masters asked me many direct and detailed questions about my career at the coffee shop. Many of the issues he sighted were not available to the general public and it made me suspect that he must have had access at some time to highly confidential police personnel documents to gain this information.

This is also an issue I wondered about when reading Mike Carlton's article in the *Sydney Morning Herald*, mentioned at the start of this chapter. In the same article, having inaccurately quoted me, Carlton said:

> *Priest alleged (Commissioner) Ryan's wife gave Mike Carlton his (Priest's) Internal Affairs record.*

I'm confused. I thought Carlton when giving evidence before the Parliamentary inquiry into Cabramatta in 2002 had said that he had discussed my Internal Affairs file with Commissioner Ryan over dinner.

Now he is reporting that I have said that Mr Ryan's wife gave Carlton my IA file. I never said that. I am, to this day, at a total loss as to how my confidential police internal files were made available to Mike Carlton.

From that point on, it was apparent to me that Clive Small was, in Masters eyes, the answer to all things policing and to suggest otherwise or offer alternate scenarios was a complete waste of time and effort.

The meeting ended amicably at the coffee shop and we parted. We later exchanged further emails and put our points of view across in more detail.

At no time did Masters tell me our coffee meeting was an interview. He should have formally told me so, it would have been the ethical thing to do.

Although Masters denied how close he and Small were, in the book *Sins of the Brothers* by Mark Whittaker and Les Kennedy:

> *Masters had known Clive Small casually for years. The cop had a reputation for being one of the good guys. Masters saw him as an interesting study, because he provided a good rebuttal to the argument put about by the old guard that all the best coppers in the force had been purged during the Avery years—they pushed the line that you needed to be a crook to fight crime.*

The 'best coppers' were still in the Force in 1994.It was not the 'purging' of John Avery but the aftermath of the Wood Royal Commission that resulted in many good cops leaving the NSW Police. It resembled the 'night of the long knives' in many instances. Good cops done over for no other reason than they were a threat to lesser performing 'academic cops' and in the case of Brian Harding, John Garvey and the other victims of the Kareela cat burglar scandal (see chapter 3), they were wrongly purged by the Wood Royal Commission.

Despite their years of dedication and service, they had become enemies of the state they had served.

If Chris Masters had done more research on Clive Small, he

would have found that in fact Small was heavily connected to the 'old guard' that he himself was criticising. He had served time at the old Breaking Squad with Detective Sergeant Brendon John Whelan, who was mentioned in Parliament by John Hatton as corrupt. Small and Whelan worked for many years on various enquiries and Royal Commissions.

Small also worked with a supposed old guard detective Rod Lynch, who, as a result of corruption allegations, was prevented from being promoted by the NSW Police Commissioner because he lacked 'integrity'. Rod Lynch appealed to a Tribunal who upheld the Commissioner's decision. It is my understanding that he was never cleared for promotion but was 'taken on board' into new Crime Agencies unit under Clive Small. Lynch was then promoted to a Senior 'Acting' rank.

Michael Drury explained to Masters at our coffee shop 'interview' the tremendous damage that had been done to not only my reputation, but also Richard Basham and Alan Jones by journalists.

After I commenced an action in the Supreme Court about the incident reported in *Jonestown* and the matter was quickly settled, Masters put out his revised edition of the book some months later. It is interesting to note that Masters in his later revised and updated version of the book, writes, 'I did not see Priest as corrupt'.

I, along with another Cabramatta Detective Sergeant Ray King, had an enviable arrest rate that ranked towards the top of all Detective Sergeant's in the State. That is not a boast. Ask any of the Detectives I worked with in the period 1996-2000, which is what Masters should have done, if this was a seriously researched tome.

Ask the brief handling manager at Fairfield Prosecutors office, where most of the briefs went. Look up the Court records for Fairfield and Burwood Courts for that period. This was Cabramatta after all, with murders, attempted murders, shootings, massive drug dealing, serious assaults, stabbings, heroin overdoses, coming at you day after day. If you were incompetent as a Detective, you would be quickly found out.

One of my 'opponents' admitted during an investigation on the disaster at Cabramatta that Priest 'made lots of arrests, the young police looked up to him because he was the old school detective, tough.'

If you make hundreds of arrests and the work just keeps coming through the door by the hour, as it did at Cabramatta and not just minor crimes, but major offences, you eventually will make a mistake and that is a fact. Not enough resources, not enough help, mistakes are made. Did I perhaps allow a serial killer co-offender escape detection because of incompetence? No I didn't.

An Internal Affairs report in 2001 lists 'dismissed prosecutions' in my career as 'a most unusual one'. I have the document.

Even with the hundreds of arrests that I made during this period, the records, which don't lie, indicated dismissed prosecutions were 'unusual'.

Alan Jones was criticised at this time for trying to stop police reform. Alan Jones is a strong supporter of the NSW Police Force. I spoke to both the Shadow Police spokesman for the NSW Opposition, Mick Gallagher, a former policeman and Malcolm Kerr, the member for Cronulla and a former DPP Lawyer. Both were unanimous in saying that Alan Jones had done more for policing and police than anyone else in New

South Wales.

Indeed on Tuesday 16 October 2001, Chris Hartcher, the member for Gosford, opposition frontbencher and a senior Liberal politician, had this to say in the NSW Parliament:

> *The Legislative Council exposed the deficiency of policing in the Cabramatta area and exploded the issue. It was Alan Jones who everyday on the radio pounded the incompetence of the Government as far as policing in New South Wales is concerned. And it was the hundreds of police who contacted Alan Jones and who contact the opposition constantly—who revealed their frustrations at the inadequacies of policing in New South Wales.....*

Many journalists including Chris Masters became focussed on my private life and linked me with Alan Jones even during my successful Supreme Court action against the NSW Police for, amongst other things, harassment and intimidation.

At that time in 2006 there had been considerable media coverage over my Supreme Court action against the NSW Police, who challenged my claim.

It is to be expected that lawyers representing the police force would take all steps necessary to protect the interests of their client. But there comes a time when lawyers legally and morally, have to admit that their clients, including the Police Department or one of its servants, has caused someone some grief, whether intentionally or not. It is well known that both judges and the community in general are critical of lawyers who take things too far and prolong cases unnecessarily.

The following are the facts as seen by His Honour, Justice

Peter Johnson of the NSW Supreme Court, who on 2 February 2007 delivered this stinging observation:

> With respect to the second issue, namely compliance by the Defendant with respect to Category 30 of the order for discovery (the diaries issue), there has been an unsatisfactory response by the Defendant to that order, part of which, I referred to, in short form, in paras 78 to 81 of my judgment on 28 November 2006. There was in my view a legitimate grievance by the plaintiff (me) with respect to the response by the defendant to compliance with category of discovery.
>
> It took further orders of the Court and an affidavit sworn this week to bring this issue to a head in a manner, which in my view was capable of earlier resolution.

My lawyers had sought and been given access to various highly confidential police documents that for various reasons the Police Department failed to produce notwithstanding an order from the Supreme Court of New South Wales.

We had sought and been given access to the 'Operation Retz' documents in February 2006, yet here we are in the early part of 2007 and they still had not supplied the documents in their entirety and in fact challenged His Honours earlier orders. But then it became very obvious why there was a problem.

The defendant had submitted to the Court on the 14 December 2006 that two lever-arched folders were the 'Operation Retz' Report. I knew it wasn't immediately, as by sheer co-incidence, the NSW Legislative Council had also got wind of the Operation Retz saga and had ordered that they be delivered to the Parliament for examination. Subsequently

40 boxes of documents arrived, not just the two lever arched folders delivered to the Supreme Court in my matter.

His Honour was not impressed:

> *Some 37 boxes, containing in excess of 100 lever arch folders (not two) were provided to my chambers yesterday following the communications from the defendant's solicitor...*
>
> *In the light of that conclusion, where does one go from here? I have two lever-arched folders, MF15. I have a failure by the defendant to comply with my first direction of 14 December 2006. I have 37 boxes delivered to my chambers, in relation to which the evidence of Mr McGillicuddy adduced today is that there is at least something in each box which relates to Operation Retz.*

How do 2 lever-arched folders turn into 37 boxes containing 100 lever-arched folders between the 14 December 2006 and February 2007? They must have multiplied over the Christmas break, 50 times over.

But it was the question of costs that ultimately were paid by the taxpayer that really hit home to the journalists assembled in the Courtroom.

> *I made it clear in my judgment of 28 November 2006 that whatever the outcome of the defendant's application to withdraw category 27 from the order for discovery, it may have to bear the costs, bearing in mind the way in which this issue has arisen. I am satisfied, on the present state of this application that an order should be made against*

the defendant with respect to costs. I have in mind, in that regard, the provisions which I have referred in s.56 Civil procedure Act 2005 and what I regard as failures on the part of the defendant to comply with its obligations to the Court revealed in the approach to litigation to date.

If the Police Legal and the Crown Solicitors Office thought that was telling, they were in for an unpleasant surprise. It got worse. Much worse.

> *...A party to civil proceedings is under a duty to assist the Court to further that overriding purpose and, to that affect, to participate in the processes of the Court and to comply with the directions and orders of that Court. S.56(3) A Solicitor or Barrister must not by his or her conduct, cause his or her client to be put in breach of the duty identified in s.56 (3): s.56 (4). ...*
>
> *In a sense, s.56 has the result that every litigant in civil proceedings in this Court is now a model litigant. However there is ample authority that Government bodies, including the Commonwealth of Australia or the State of New South Wales, ought to be regarded as having model litigant obligations extending in the past, at least, beyond those of private litigants.....*
>
> *I am not satisfied, given the history that I have recited in this judgment, that the defendant has discharged it's obligations under s.56 Civil Procedures Act 2005, or indeed it's model litigant obligations with respect to the category 27 issue.*
>
> *Section 89 Civil Procedures Act 2005 provides that costs are the discretion of the Court. Costs may be ordered on*

an ordinary basis or an indemnity basis. In my view, the approach of the Defendant to this application to date, and to compliance with orders of the Court, is such that there has not been just, quick and cheap resolution of the issues falling for determination. Indeed there has been a continuing inability of the Court to discharge its functions because he has not complied with its obligations.

His Honour went on to award costs on an 'indemnity basis' to me against the defendant in the litigation. Courts rarely make costs orders on an indemnity basis and do so to punish a party that has simply failed to carry out procedural steps in a timely and efficient manner. It is extraordinary that in proceedings in which the Crown Solicitor's office and Police Legal were representing the interests of the police department, for an indemnity costs order to be made, particularly given the Crown Solicitor's office obligation to be a 'model litigant'.

It wasn't just in his book that Masters displayed an interest in my private life. Launching *Jonestown* on ABC television's *7.30 Report* with long time friend and colleague, Kerry O'Brien, Masters was barely into the interview when he mentioned my name and my compensation claim, which was at that time still before the courts. He told Kerry that there was a lack of 'transparency' in my claim, and suggested again that it was Alan Jones's power that was behind it.

Yes the Government did settle out of court and yes they most certainly did save a considerable amount of 'exposure' to tax payers' dollars by not having the matter progress to trial. The terms are confidential but nevertheless details were leaked to the media, the *Sydney Morning Herald*'s political editor Andrew Clennell who did an article in 2007 on the barely one-month-old confidential settlement.

Clennell's article lacked balance. He refers to me constantly hanging up on the *Herald* as though that was an indication that I was hiding something sinister and trying to avoid probing questions. Yet, unfairly, Clennell, didn't report the fact that I was bound by a confidentiality clause which had been endorsed by the Supreme Court of NSW which was the reason I kept hanging up. I later rang a senior *Herald* journalist and complained. He agreed that it was unfair and that he had spoken to Clennell about it. Clennell never bothered to write a clarifying retraction. But who did tell Clennell about the terms of the settlement?

I have pondered over the theory that Masters in the 1990s and 2000s and into the present decade got too close to certain police and followed their information without enough examination of alternate facts. It's one thing to complain about the defamation risks of modern investigative journalism, it's another thing to keep making errors of fact that can only end up in the defamation courts.

Second, I find it difficult to reconcile the change in Master's attitude to me after the coffee shop 'interview' in 2006.

My life was changed irrevocably by the media's relentless treatment of me.

It seems the only thing that really can regulate what is published is costly and time-consuming defamation proceedings, which at the end of the day can only ever impose a financial disincentive.

The use of unnamed sources was a feature in some articles critical of me. Paul Sheehan, the Fairfax journalist, in his book, *The Electronic Whorehouse*, describes the practice of using unnamed sources to put forward a damaging statement:

If someone is willing to be quoted in the story, but unwilling to be named, it raises the obvious question: who is using whom?

6.

UNDER THE RADAR:
THE WINCHESTER CASE

In January 1989, in a Canberra suburb, Australian Federal Police Assistant Commissioner Colin Winchester had just returned home. As he was getting out of his car he was shot dead.

A subsequent probe by journalist Chris Masters into the Colin Winchester murder raises yet another interesting case of investigative journalists becoming quasi police investigators operating without the restraints, and in many cases the experience, of operational police on the ground.

How do journalists go under the radar, undetected and unaccountable for their actions? What happens when information, given to them by an unnamed source is used to publically criticise individuals with little regard for the consequences to those individuals when that information is found to be fantasy?

Chris Masters' program within Channel 10's current affairs series *Page One* had an initial episode titled *A Capital Murder*. It went to air on 24 April 1989 with a related episode screened a week later on 1 May.

The episode concerned the murder of Colin Winchester, a much loved and admired policeman in the old ACT Police and subsequently when it merged with the Commonwealth Police to become what is today the Australian Federal Police (AFP). Chris Masters' report said:

> *On January 10 this year in Canberra, Australian Assistant Commissioner Colin Winchester, was assassinated. The shot, heard around the world, has provoked deafness among some Police because, to thoroughly investigate the Winchester murder, is to reveal matters which some Police would prefer to remain hidden.*

It was absolutely guaranteed to have everyone sitting at the edge of their couch. Then followed this:

> *Nobody likes to speak ill of the dead, especially when their end is sudden and brutal. There is no doubt that behind the official public eulogies, there was real private grief. But also in private, there were whispers that Winchester was corrupt. Politicians were briefed to be cautious. Honest policeman, the rumours went, don't get assassinated. On the other hand, crooked policeman aren't normally this popular. To his close friends, there was no way that Winchester was bent.*

The source for the whispers is not given. The anonymous

'informant' is not named.

In many ways, the investigative journalist should be like a detective, seeking the truth and presenting evidence of fact not fiction. Where the two differ is in control. The detective is governed by rules of evidence, strict controls set by the parliament, the courts and his superiors. Journalists are supposed to abide by a code of ethics but breaches of that are rarely punished or so it seems, unless they or their publisher are sued for defamation in the courts.

When was the last time a journalist was 'struck off' or banned because of a flawed story?

Masters in his program went on to list suspects for the Winchester murder, who included the mafia, a Canberra public servant (who was the main suspect from very early on in the case) and a 'new' suspect, delivered up by none other than Masters himself, courtesy of a 'source'.

> *The other [suspect] was not being investigated at all, not, that is, until I interviewed him last week. There is good reason for that. He is none other than the man who was leading the Winchester investigation, Commander Lloyd Worthy.*

At that moment, Chris Masters 'revealed' on national television that the very police officer in charge of the investigation into the murder was now a suspect, albeit, through Chris Masters himself via an unnamed source.

The quest was on to find the murderer of Winchester. It was one of the most high profile murder investigations in the country for decades. But now, through the allegations of a Channel 10 journalist on information provided by an unidentified 'source', that investigation was diverted.

As the program progressed, Masters spoke, with some authority and accuracy, on the bitter rivalry between the old ACT Police and the new Commonwealth Police, who had been amalgamated into the Australian Federal Police (AFP).

> *Rivalry was at its most intense just before the amalgamation, and came to a head at a hotel just down the road from Parliament House. Pine Lodge briefly became notorious.*
>
> *In a secret room was an illegal casino. Pine Lodge [casino] became a haunt for the ACT Police and this attracted the attention of the Commonwealth Police. They [Commonwealth Police] believed, that to stay open, Pine Lodge must be receiving protection from the ACT Police.*

Who was the source for that information? When Masters continued, he dropped yet another bombshell:

> *Page One has learned that the Commonwealth Police received important evidence that Inspector First Class Colin Winchester of the ACT Police collected a substantial bribe from Pine Lodge.*

Masters reported that a mafia figure was allegedly dealing the cards at this illegal casino. Here is a combination of allegations that involve alleged mafia figures, drugs, illegal casinos and alleged bribes to police officers. What evidence did Masters have? Was he shown that evidence? Was it formally tendered into any proceedings against Winchester?

These allegations were ones that Colin Winchester's family would find difficult to disprove, especially as they were still grieving the loss of a husband and father. Did someone have something substantive in the form of 'evidence' as Masters put it?

I am certain that had 'evidence' existed of that fact Colin Winchester would never have advanced to Assistant Commissioner. Where was Chris Masters taking both the viewer and the police investigating Winchester's murder?

Further on into the program Chris Masters speculated that after repeated enquiries, he was able to establish that Winchester, may have taken a bribe, not for himself, but a superior officer. Then he states that, 'the Winchester bribe was never resolved'. Maybe it was never resolved because it never happened. And resolved for whom? The grieving Winchester family on learning of this allegation?

Masters then turned his attention onto another former ACT Police Officer leading the investigation, Lloyd Worthy. Like Winchester, Lloyd Worthy was a rugged, tough, no nonsense Detective. Highly regarded not only by fellow ACT Police but also interstate police, Worthy was also a superb athlete, a representative rugby league player and a quality ballistics-trained detective. You don't get much better than that in the police force.

However, Masters said:

Immediately after the interview, I presented the Federal Police with information which has caused them to remove Commander Worthy from the inquiry. He is now under investigation himself.......If Winchester told Worthy that afternoon that it was to be acted upon, and I have no evidence that this happened, it could be construed as a motive for murder.

Masters interviewed Worthy on the program over a 'matter' that 'could affect his career'. It was obvious from the answers Lloyd Worthy gave that he had not the slightest idea what Masters was talking about.

Chris Masters: Can I ask you what you were doing at the time of the murder?
Lloyd Worthy: Of course, I was at home with my family and I had a telephone call that Mr. Winchester had been shot and I immediately went to his home.

The fact that Lloyd Worthy answered that phone in the presence of his family should have required only the most cursory inquiry to counter Masters' allegations. But operating on those allegations, the Australian Federal Police appointed a 'team' to investigate Commander Lloyd Worthy. They stood down Lloyd Worthy from his duties on the murder, stripping the Task Force of its leader. You can just imagine the chaos that must have caused an already stressed and pressured team of detectives on the case. Masters went on to boast that:

Teams of dozens of detectives, spending hundreds of thousands of dollars, did not discover this 'evidence' for 13 long weeks....'

Further on, to give credence to his allegations:

> It's not so surprising that a suspect could emerge from
> within the Force.

Now we have a suspect, who emerged, courtesy of 'whisper'.
Masters went on:

> The murder must be thoroughly investigated. There can
> be no shadow of a cover-up. Assistant Commissioner Colin
> Winchester deserves better than that.

Winchester, most certainly did deserve better than that. And
Lloyd Worthy also deserved better than what he got. On
a subsequent follow up *Page One* program that was titled:
'Doubts expressed over AFP handling of investigations into the
murder of Assistant Commissioner Colin Winchester.' Chris
Masters again:

> The issue reached an extremity with the arrival on the
> scene of this man, Commander Lloyd Worthy.
> Worthy was the Chief Investigator on the Winchester
> murder. Largely because of information discovered by Page
> One, he is now being investigated himself.
> The Federal Police chose to take Worthy off the case and
> investigate Worthy, not 'Page One'.

What did Masters expect the AFP to do after he, Masters, publicly
examined the motives and whereabouts of the Team Leader of
the Winchester murder enquiry, on national television?

Masters was treading a fine line and placing himself at risk of being charged with public mischief. If Masters had gone privately to the AFP murder enquiry team and gave them the information that he had from his 'source', that would have been appropriate and dignified. No. He chose to go on national television and 'air' his allegations in public.

Of course, Lloyd Worthy was entirely innocent and he sued Masters in the civil courts and won.

Lloyd Worthy was soon cleared of suspicion in any of the matters raised by Masters. He retired after 38 dedicated years with the ACT Police and then the AFP. Despite his great ability and dedication, Lloyd Worthy remained on the rank of Commander for the rest of his service after the allegations raised on *Page One*. He deserved better than that and so did the community. He is now prominently involved with helping troubled youth reclaim their lives with the Outward Bound program.

Colin Winchester is still revered by the many police that knew him and were privileged to have worked with him, along with the many citizens he touched over an outstanding police career.

On Wednesday 24 May 1989, the *Capitol Murder* segment was raised in the Australian Parliament. Senator Tate said:

A week or so ago Senator Lewis asked me a question concerning allegations against Commander Lloyd Worthy made on the Page One program on television put together by Chris Masters. I think it was put to Mr. Worthy by Chris Masters that he—that is, Mr. Worthy—could be a suspect for the murder of Assistant Commissioner Colin Winchester.

I have some supplementary information which might be of interest to Honourable Senators.

As a consequence of these allegations Commander Worthy was transferred to other duties and an investigation was initiated into the allegations. The investigation was undertaken by Commander Allen and Detective Superintendent Lewington of the National Criminal Investigation Branch, AFP Headquarters. The investigation has now been completed and a full report has been made available to me. In essence, the investigation by the AFP headquarters officers has confirmed that at the time Assistant Commissioner Winchester was murdered, Commander Worthy was at home with his wife and family. In negation of suspicion of any involvement it has been established that there was no argument or conflict between Commander Worthy and Assistant Commissioner Winchester and no other motive or circumstances that could give rise to the slightest suspicion that Commander Worthy was responsible for or involved in the death of Assistant Commissioner Winchester. Commander Worthy has now returned to his former duties as Officer in Charge, ACT region, Crime Division. That is the briefing provided to me by Deputy Commissioner John Johnson.

Commander Worthy was the subject of an allegation which one can hardly imagine could be more damaging or destructive to the professional career or reputation of a Police Officer. The thought that he might even countenance, let alone be involved in, the murder of Assistant Commissioner Winchester was of course extremely damaging to him.

While the civil courts vindicated Lloyd Worthy, to this day Chris Masters has never been brought to account by any public authority. Where did Masters get his information that encouraged him to make such a baseless allegation?

In November 1989, some 10 months after the murder, the initial suspect, David Eastman was convicted and sentenced to life imprisonment for killing Colin Winchester at his home. The investigation team deserves enormous praise for the way they went about their job despite the pressure and the needless sidetracking caused by one member of the media.

Police corruption was, and still is a concern, no matter how limited that corruption is in terms of the number of police involved and the type of offences committed. The correct forum for investigating corruption allegations is not via the media.

Another example that exposes the lack of public restraints on journalists occurred in 2001. This concerns an extraordinary public hearing at the Police Integrity Commission in Sydney on Monday, 8 October 2001.

Justice Wood had only finished delivering his final Wood Royal Commission Report into Police Corruption to the New South Wales Parliament 1997, some four years previously. The Police Integrity Commission was designed to display revolutionary, new police anti corruption measures that would take the form of long-running and intensive investigations, with telephone intercepts, listening devices, covert cameras and undercover police trapping suspect fellow police. It had all the hallmarks of a major 'sting' you more readily relate to drug importations and other serious organised crime cases.

The corruption probe began with the co-operation of New

South Wales Police Internal Affairs and the New South Wales Crime Commission and ran for nearly three years without being detected by any of the police or criminals involved. That in itself was a major breakthrough—no leaks, no warning calls to cops doing dirty business. In a nutshell they were caught cold and most of them deserved to be.

The film footage of cops taking cash, stealing property and cavorting with heroin dealers was not pretty. It was a shameful day in New South Wales Policing. Fortunately, those days have become fewer and fewer as the years pass.

At that time in 2001, the then New South Wales Police Commissioner, Peter Ryan, was at the political cross roads as to whether he was going to be sacked by an increasingly frustrated Carr Government, itself feeling the pressure from a demoralized Police Force and a very suspicious public as to the true state of crime in New South Wales.

Chris Masters from the ABC *Four Corners* program, interviewed Peter Ryan. The resulting documentary in 2001 showed that police corruption still existed, that Peter Ryan was still in charge and he was the rock that stood between police corruption and the 'new' police force. He wanted to be known, in his own words, as 'the thief taker', which is a British policing term for what is a normal day to day job for police all over the world; locking up crooks.

When Peter Ryan first became New South Wales Police Commissioner in 1996 he was instrumental in the controversial axing of the New South Wales Police Board that had been a reasonably effective overseer to the position of Police Commissioner. Ryan created a new body that had distinctly less control, in fact none, over the management of the Police

Force and created another committee in the State of New South Wales called The Commissioner's Advisory Group.

The CAG was designed to help the new Commissioner take command of the Police Service. The group included Dr Richard Basham, The Director of Public Prosecutions, Nicholas Cowdery and several other notable people including Chris Masters of the ABC. Richard Basham kept notes of the CAG meetings. On the first meeting he sat directly opposite Chris Masters. I am not aware of how many more meetings Masters attended.

The fact that a journalist was on the Police Commissioners Advisory Group always troubled me and still does. I presume that Masters would have informed Ryan that if a critical story on the New South Wales Police Service came his way as an investigative reporter working for the publicly funded *Four Corners* program, he would resign his position on the group immediately, thereby ensuring the integrity of the group and himself.

Luckily for both Masters and Ryan, this situation did not appear to arise during Ryan's controversial leadership of the New South Wales Police. That was until Masters interviewed Ryan for the *Operation Florida* program. At that time Chris Masters was also approved by the New South Wales Crime Commission and the Police Integrity Commission to exclusively report on the operation.

The New South Wales Crime Commission is an extremely secretive body. There are always stringent integrity checks amongst police that are seconded there for various 'references' or 'strike forces' on a temporary and self-limiting basis. If one of those cops had published or was about to publish a book, and in that book they disclosed an association with a known criminal,

I am certain they would have been immediately excluded from having any contact with the NSW Crime Commission.

Chris Masters did indeed write a book that came out in 2002 after the broadcast of Master's program on Operation Florida.

That book was called *Not for Publication*. In it a chapter called 'My Gangster' discloses several things that concerned Michael Drury, a New South Wales undercover drug squad cop and colleague of mine for many years in the NSW Police and me.

In *Not for Publication*, Masters discloses that he had a mate, who he refers to as 'my gangster', and the chapter details the 'alleged' activities of 'my gangster' cutting the legs off a harmless but yelping poodle on board a harbour cruise in front of its owner and then shooting the decapitated and agonized dog. Or 'my gangster' slicing the Achilles tendon of an adolescent youth who just happened to irritate 'my gangster' whilst he was out riding a bike—a catastrophic medical event for a young maturing man I would think and at the very least warranting a charge of Malicious Wounding and a substantial prison term.

A lot of people were shocked that he would not only socialize with a 'gangster' but also openly write about it in a book published by the ABC.

Masters went further to disclose in the chapter, that both he and his wife became friendly with Mr and Mrs Gangster on a social basis. So what Masters alludes to as an association that began only so that Masters could gain knowledge of the underworld presumably to help with his journalism. It then developed into social meetings with Mr and Mrs Gangster. Did Chris Masters disclose to the Crime Commission and the Police Integrity Commission that he had an association with a known criminal and that they met socially with their families?

I am curious as to whether Masters divulged this relationship to the Police Commissioner Peter Ryan during his tenure on the Commissioners Advisory Group.

During 2001, Chris Masters had access to the inner workings of Police Internal Affairs, The New South Wales Crime Commission, The Police Integrity Commission and Commissioner Peter Ryan. The scene was set for a blockbuster, with Peter Ryan starring as the 'the thief taker', directed by Chris Masters.

The first day of the hearings at the Police Integrity Commission arrived on 8 October 2001 and the witnesses, some voluntary, some not so, walked through the crowds including the media who were filming the arrival of the 'offenders' at the PIC Hearing rooms. How the camera crews were always able to identify the alleged corrupt police walking towards the St James Centre always intrigued me. Do cameraman and reporters have a sixth sense like the great detectives of the past? Or were there 'spotters' in the crowd making sure the 'offenders' were duly identified before they were to give evidence.

The hearings were a sellout, packed mostly by the media who witnessed extraordinary segments of evidence, including videotapes of police openly engaging in corruption along with civilian drug dealers. Listening device and telephone intercepts of the corruption were a feature of the PIC show on one particular day, 8 October 2001.

Another 'show' began at 8.30pm that same evening, 8 October 2001, on the ABC on the Chris Masters led *Four Corners* program, with the title 'Directing Traffic'. The episode included corruption, drugs, crooks, a solicitor here and there, crooked cops, cop talk. The 'evidence' shown was impressive, from a police point of view, and the cops were caught red handed, mostly.

During the airing of the program a number of criminal offences appear to have been committed by the assembled cast of crooked cops, drug dealers and the odd solicitor.

The agreement between Masters/*Four Corners*, the PIC, the Crime Commission and the New South Wales Police on running a program on national television had included the proviso that any material broadcast had to have already been given in evidence before the Police Integrity Commission, thereby becoming exempt under the various acts of Parliament. This is set out clearly in the Report by the Inspector of the PIC into the *Four Corners* program.

In other words, Masters could show material that had already been given in evidence before the PIC and then he was, with certain limitations, free to air that evidence. That was the game plan but somewhere along the way, the plan fell apart. Masters and the ABC aired material that HAD NOT been given in evidence that day and potentially damaged a future prosecution of corrupt police and an associate, a solicitor.

The airing of the material had significant impact on future court matters, as well as the cost of such proceedings either folding or worse still, not being commenced at all, because of this mistake.

If that material is not exempt, and there is some discussion as to whether telephone intercept material is ever exempt in any circumstances, and that material is broadcast, it is a criminal offence under Parliamentary Acts such as the Police Integrity Act, The Crime Commission Act, The Telecommunications

(Intercepts) Act and the Listening Devices Act etc.

It may be a 'technical' offence, but an offence nonetheless and justice should not only be done, but seen to be done.

The following excerpts from *Hansard* on 16 October 2001 show both the Government and the Opposition trading blows over the *Four Corners* episode. The debate was led chiefly by the former Opposition Shadow Police Minister, Andrew Tink:

Andrew Tink: My question is directed to the Minister for Police. Has the Minister asked the Commissioner of Police whether he, or anyone on his behalf, provided secretly taped evidence of police corruption exclusively to the Four Corners program which was broadcast before such evidence was tendered to the Police Integrity Commission hearing, thus breaching the Police Code of Conduct and clearly being in contempt of the PIC?

Paul Whelan: I am advised that Four Corners was given access to the material screened last Monday night in co-operation with the Police Integrity Commission, the Crime Commission and the Police Service.

Later in Parliamentary proceedings that day the debate became entertaining:

Andrew Tink: I am utterly astonished if what the Minister said in the house this afternoon is right, that the Police Integrity Commission was involved in green lighting information being given on an exclusive basis to the Four Corners program. To put this in context, Four Corners showed a number of secret tapes indicating corruption and

criminality of the worst type, one of which at least was not at
the time it went to air on the Four Corners program entered
into evidence before the Police Integrity Commission. It
was a taped conversation between a Solicitor Mr...... and
B5, [PIC codename] recorded on 14 November 2000. The
transcript, exhibit 65 and the tape itself, exhibit 64, were not
entered into evidence before the Police Integrity Commission
until Tuesday 9 October 2001, as is shown by the transcript
of that day. A tape of Mr...... and B5 had been entered on
the previous day, being exhibits 5 and 6, but that tape was
not the tape of Mr...... and B5 shown on Monday evening on
the Four Corners program.

It was a well-constructed question on the chain of events that
followed the airing of the *Four Corners* program on Operation
Florida. It seemed to a number of parliamentarians present
that day, that a prima facie case existed (and still exists) of an
offence, initially under the Police Integrity Act, then later under
further Acts of Parliament, perhaps the Telecommunications
Act (Intercepts) and the Listening Devices Act. Andrew Tink
continued:

I have spoken to every one of my colleagues on the
Opposition benches and we are, to a person, all incredibly
troubled by this course of conduct by the Government, the
Police Integrity Commission, the Crime Commission and
the Police Commissioner. What is going on? What is the
agenda? The Leader of the Opposition reminded me that
in this House this afternoon the Police Minister talked at
great length about the incredible secrecy surrounding the

investigation that took place. When did Four Corners program get all of these incredibly secret tapes? How many days or weeks before they were entered into evidence were the tapes made available to people at the ABC? Who had them? 'What happened to them? What arrangements were made for security'?

The many questions Andrew Tink asked were extremely damaging to the Government and its then Police Minister, Paul Whelan. Tink later asked another question about the circumstances of *Four Corners* being 'chosen' to do the Operation Florida program.

One third of the members of the lower house want an explanation about why the ABC made a special deal and saw those tapes before they were entered into evidence. What was the agenda? What was the arrangement? What was the security?

The Police media policy has been breached because one media outlet had exclusive access to the most sensitive, extraordinary evidence which, at the time of the broadcast, had yet to be entered into evidence. Why has the code of conduct been breached? It has been with the knowledge and concurrence of the Police Integrity Commission, how does the commission explain itself to every Police Officer who is enjoined repeatedly to abide by the conduct'?

Is it only certain people, say police below the rank of Commissioner, that have to abide by the media policy and code of conduct?

Perhaps some of the answers lay in Andrew Tink's following remarks:

How could that, if the Minister is to be believed, acting partially to one broadcaster as distinct from others? Heaven knows what sort of quid pro quo was involved. We would like to find out, by the way and I think the minister owes it to everyone to explain why.

The Police Integrity Commission which must, above everything, in an enquiry of this gravity, act with complete impartiality to be signing off on the handling of this material to one media outlet for what appeared to me to be a pretty soft interview with the Police Commissioner. It was followed up on the subsequent Friday, I might add, by the interviewer (Masters) himself being interviewed on Stateline defending the Police Commissioner of a management problem, doing a great job.

Let us open it up. Let us have some openness. Let us have some transparency about what has gone on, because until this issue is clarified the credibility of this inquiry (Florida) is at stake. It is a breach of conduct and breach of police media policy. He has acted partially in favor of one media outlet compared with others. There have been some pretty soft interviews, it appears, in connection with this material that has been broadcast. Why? What is the deal? Why the soft interviews with one media outlet?

Soon, what started out as being a good news story for Commissioner Ryan was turned on its head by the revelations on *Four Corners* of material that was not put into evidence.

Thereby the subplot of how that material was released to the media became bigger than the main plot of police corruption. Peter Ryan's opportunity for public recognition was derailed.

There were further exchanges between both sides of the NSW Parliament that followed much the same pattern until this:

> *Andrew Tink: You, Minister, are responsible, at the end of the day, for the whole lot of it. They report to you. The Commissioner of Police reports to you. You ought to be long gone. You ought to go off and make a full time job of your pubs. Stop running the conflict of interest. Just go and run the pubs, run the horses, enjoy the surf at Wamberal. Whatever you do just get out of here. Give a new minister a go.*
>
> *Paul Whelan: You are attacking the PIC.*
>
> *For seven long years opposition members have been involved in a concerted campaign, denying there was corruption in the Police Service and still is. In the halcyon days of the Liberal Party and the National Party running the Police Service, Chook Fowler, Trevor Haken and a whole list were held up as examples. Tim Priest can be quoted about the current state of integrity in the Police Service. At Page 20 (Cabramatta Inquiry 2001) of the transcript he said that integrity issues in the Police Service now are higher than they have ever been.*
>
> *Mr. Oakshott: He has had to resign.*
>
> *Paul Whelan: It was a voluntary decision. He does not have to go; he has been asked by the Commissioner to stay.*

I did go. Some ten months later, medically discharged. But I managed to work under Michael Costa as Police Minister for nearly six months, and that six months contained some of the best days of my police service.

Costa did try to bring about real change and quickly, too quickly for some, and he was later shifted out of the police portfolio in 2002 to handle an equal Ministerial train wreck, the Transport Ministry.

It was a tragedy for the police force and the community that Costa was never allowed to implement more of his changes, changes that basically came from within the Police Force and the community, rather than the so called 'crime experts' based at various 'safe houses' called universities.

Soon Paul Whelan would come under enormous criticism over his and the government's handling of the troubled Cabramatta Police Patrol, the acknowledged heroin capital and probably the homicide capital of Australia as well.

Ray Martin in 2001 did a highly acclaimed segment on the 60 Minutes program on the massive problems confronting police in Cabramatta. He interviewed me and other players in the Cabramatta saga. He also interviewed Police Minister Paul Whelan, who having returned recently from overseas, was obviously not at his best. When Ray Martin asked the Police Minister if he had visited Cabramatta recently, the hapless Minister replied, 'I have been meaning to but I haven't got around to it yet'.

It was akin to a US journalist asking the US Army's Commanding Officer if he had visited Baghdad after the invasion. Can you imagine the general saying, 'I have been meaning to but I haven't got around to it yet.'

Whether Paul Whelan realized it or not at the time, the scandal of corruption revealed by Operation Florida and the Cabramatta interview saw the challenge put out by Andrew Tink in Parliament for Whelan to go soon eventuate. Whelan lasted a short time before being replaced by Michael Costa in 2001.

The government stumbled over the opposition's sustained attack and did everything but answer Andrew Tink's questions.

What was Paul Whelan and the government to do?

Shortly after, the Inspector of the Police Integrity Commission, who oversees the running of the PIC, wrote to the Commissioner of the Police Integrity Commission about his concerns over the motion of censure moved by Andrew Tink in Parliament the day before.

The Inspector, His Honour Justice Mervyn Finlay QC, wrote:

What troubles me in particular is the circumstance of the Four Corners program being provided with material, including taped evidence, which had not at the time it was provided and then broadcast on the 8 October, 2001 been presented as evidence in the hearing. Was such material divulged in accordance with a direction following certification under Section 56(4) of the Police Integrity Commission Act that it was in the public interest to do so.

After viewing a draft response to his initial letter, Finlay wrote on the 23 October 2001:

The question remains, what went wrong? If the Commission had effectively made arrangements so that they would know what material supplied by them was to be broadcast on the night of 8 October 2001, why could it not have ensured that such material was tendered in evidence during that day in the course of the opening? That, as I see it, remains a major issue.

At the time of writing this book in early 2009, it still remains a major issue and is still unresolved. And this is despite the powerful investigative tools at the disposal of the Police Integrity Commission, the New South Wales Crime Commission and the New South Wales Police Force.

I have sifted through volumes of reports, transcripts and investigations conducted in the wake of this debacle and it appears to me on the face of this material that no one has ever bothered to interview, formally, Chris Masters or anyone connected with the ABC, over the Operation Florida media disclosure.

Having read the material concerning the 'recruiting' of Chris Masters to the Operation Florida segment, the PIC took the view that the program offered a chance to deter corrupt police from operating in New South Wales.

Whether that was a wise or justified view is open to discussion. Certainly PIC Assistant Commissioner Tim Sage, who was running the hearing, thought so after much legal debate within the PIC over such action. I have great regard for Tim Sage, having worked alongside him at the National Crime Authority on the Italian Organized Crime reference. Sage was a senior lawyer attached to our team and he was a highly competent and knowledgeable lawyer with immense personal integrity. Whatever decision Tim Sage made in this case would have been carefully considered. Indeed Chris Masters and his team signed undertakings that they would:

Abide by all order, direction and requests of the Police Integrity Commission in relation to materials supplied by the Commission.

Undertake not to further disseminate any material supplied to (him) other than with the express leave of the Commissioner;

Acknowledge that to act otherwise than in accordance with the order of the Commission is an offence pursuant to the Police Integrity Commission Act and that (He) may be liable to prosecution for any such act.

Further correspondence to Masters warning him of the restrictions by law of using material under the Telecommunications (Intercepts) Act on his program were sent not once but three times by the Police Integrity Commission.

Chris Masters appears to have been well aware of the restrictions of TI (telephone intercepts) product. Critically in Justice Finlay's report in paragraph 25 is this:

Mr. Masters was informed that notwithstanding that he had been afforded access to TI (Telephone Intercept) product prior to the commencement of Operation Florida hearings, insofar as he desired to broadcast some of this information on his Four Corners program, he would only be permitted to make use of information that had been first exhibited in hearings of the commission. At no time did the commission provide Mr. Masters or members of the his Four Corners team with permission to broadcast any TI product it had provided other than that adduced in evidence before the commission.

In closing his report, His Honour indicated that the Police Integrity Commission 'may wish' to interview Masters and that he (His Honour) would wait until that had been done before he might interview Masters as well.

I could find nothing further in the material that I read that indicated Masters was interviewed by anyone in any of the oversight bodies.

Importantly, His Honour found that tape conversation between Mr...and B5 had not been exhibited into evidence before the PIC when it went to air on *Four Corners* and:

> *As to paragraph 34, I am not satisfied that the Commission was a party to a breach of the TI Act.*

This matter had the potential to cause significant legal damage to forthcoming prosecutions, let alone stain the integrity of anti corruption bodies such as the Police Integrity Commission and to a lesser extent the New South Wales Crime Commission. Did either the Police Integrity Commission or the New South Wales Police send this information to the Director of Public Prosecutions? If not, why not?

In the current atmosphere of requiring absolute integrity by police officers at all times, investigative journalists and the oversight bodies themselves have to look at least like they are trying to play the same game.

7.
TRUE CRIME?

My own experience in policing has been that the media is as much a part of a policeman's career as his ability to fight criminals is. When I spoke out about policing in Cabramatta, I felt the full force of the media's gaze. Some journalists understood what it was that I was saying. Some, however, brought their own personal agenda to the policing debate, and their own personal judgments. And in the tight networks that make up the city of Sydney, connections with the media can make all the difference.

Mike Carlton has been in the Sydney media for over 40 years and began his career with the ABC. Carlton wrote for the The Sydney Morning Herald until they parted company in 2008. His weekly articles were described by the SMH as 'required reading' for that paper's Saturday edition. But Carlton found he was no longer 'required' when he parted ways with Fairfax during a journalists' strike.

Together with Sandy Aloisi, Mike Carlton hosts radio 2UE's drive-time program in direct opposition to Alan Jones. Carlton's ratings are about a third of Alan Jones' and that has not sat well with the former *Sydney Morning Herald* and ABC journalist.

Many years ago I was a fan of Mike Carlton. His satire was both funny and informative. But his apparent obsession with Alan Jones knows no bounds and Carlton rarely lets a week pass by without passing remarks, always unflattering, about Jones and his many achievements.

Carlton's interest in policing seems recent. My research points Carlton out as more of a political and current affairs journalist, rather than a grass roots police hound.

In 2001, Peter Ryan had been Police Commissioner for some five years and was almost a daily feature somewhere in the Sydney media. Chris Masters was an admirer of the former British bobby and both Alan Jones and John Laws often interviewed Ryan in the 2UE studios.

In early 2001, Mike Carlton initially appeared to have a grasp on the Cabramatta policing issues with the criticism of policing and crime in Cabramatta. Somehow this changed dramatically towards the end of 2001, when Carlton and the Police Commissioner appeared to become dinner partners.

What's doing today? Well good heavens, the Premier has admitted that maybe the police effort fighting drugs and crime in Cabramatta wasn't everything it should be over the last couple of years. Some police may have taken their eye off the ball, he says. Fancy that. What a surprise. Huh, who would have thought it?

It's taken the Government an awful long time to admit it,

hasn't it. Like pulling teeth. I can't think how many interviews I've done about crime in Cabramatta over the years. Dozens I would think. And all the time we're officially assured that everything's under control, the police are winning the war. Operation this had been started up and task force that had been formed and crime in Cabramatta, well, it was the media sensationalizing everything, da, da, da, da.

And now it's not. This I think, must give some satisfaction to the few brave honest police officers who had the courage to speak out, to blow the whistle. To tell the public what was really going on. Officers like Detective Sergeant Tim Priest for example, who put his career on the line to tell a parliamentary committee that police work in Cabramatta was a shambles, that gang warfare was on the rise and so on and so on and so on.

And what did he get for his troubles? He and other officers who supported him were savaged by the Police hierarchy and the government and the local Labor MP for Cabramatta, that stupid Reba Meagher. Airily dismissed Detective Sergeant Priest as a disgruntled detective. Oh, he's just a disgruntled detective, she said...I wonder if Reba Meagher would now care to come on the radio to repeat that or explain why she said it or if her views have changed, perhaps...Anxious to hear from you to justify that statement that detective Sergeant Priest was just a disgruntled detective. Bet you're not game.

We are gradually starting to get a hint, a glimmer of truth about the failure of the Police to deal with drugs and crime in Cabramatta...It certainly backs up the claims made by that copper who used to work out there—Detective Sergeant Tim

Priest. The bloke who blew the whistle to that Parliamentary Committee and warned of escalating violence and the apparent shambles of the police operation and confinement.

Remember that? A lot of that. They tried to come down on him like a ton of bricks, too, didn't they...There you have it. Wonderful, isn't it? It is apparent now that Tim Priest and those other officers who gave evidence were spot on with their warning that the Police effort at Cabramatta was in disarray. And they spoke out honestly because they couldn't take it anymore. And what will happen to their careers. I do not know. They ought to get a medal.

Mike Carlton 2UE at 3.08pm, 12 July 2001.

About an hour into that program, Carlton continued with an interview with the former Opposition Police Spokesman, Andrew Tink.

Carlton: What do you think?

Tink: I think to put this beyond all doubt the Premier owes on behalf of the whole Government, he owes Tim Priest a personal apology and he should deliver it to him. And he should also thank Tim Priest for coming forward, giving evidence to the committee and really providing a framework for this Cabramatta package that the governments now going forward with.

Carlton: It wasn't just Tim Priest though was it, I mean there were half a dozen.

Tink: Absolutely. There were five of them, Mike. It was Tim Priest who, of course has been named and identified...

Carlton: Presumably at some risk to their careers?

Tink: At great risk to their careers...

Carlton: But you would recall the concerted effort to rubbish Priest and these other officers, to dismiss them in the words of that silly Reba Meagher, as a disgruntled detective...

Yeah. There was also an effort by Senior Police to discredit Tim Priest as well, wasn't there?

Tink: I think there has been an effort at just about every level to try and put Tim Priest off what he has been saying. I'm pleased to say it has not succeeded. Priest has persevered, with a lot of guts and I think even though he still is not getting no credit for this from the government, I think the public is giving him great credit...

Carlton: All right. These remarks from the Premier today, are they a tacit admission at least...A reluctant tacit admission that Priest was right?

The interview continued. Carlton defended me against the 'rubbishing' that I had got from various key players in both government and the Police Department.

Fast forward to 2002. At this time, Carlton began socializing with Peter Ryan and Clive Small. At the same time there was a well-publicised shift from 2UE to 2GB by Alan Jones. With Carlton remaining at 2UE, the two radio journalists were in competition.

On 6 February, 2002, Michael Costa became the NSW Police Minister, Peter Ryan was on his last legs as Police Commissioner and Deputy Commissioner Ken Moroney was Commissioner in waiting.

That same year, Clive Small, the former head of Greater Hume

Region, had just been overlooked for the highly coveted position of Deputy Commissioner of Police in favour of Andrew Scipione and Dave Madden. Traditionally, one Deputy Commissioner becomes Commissioner of Police when that vacancy arises. So both Scipione and Madden were in the driving seat to become Commissioner of Police one day—indeed Andrew did succeed Ken Moroney as Commissioner in 2008.

Small would later apply for the Commissioner's job with another former senior police officer, Paul McKinnon, and the successful applicant Ken Moroney.

Soon after the Deputy Commissioner positions were filled, the subject of a replacement for the position of policy adviser on crime and community issues at the Premier's Department came up and according to Police Minister Michael Costa, his Chief of Staff, the highly regarded John Whelan, nephew of Paul Whelan, offered the position to Clive Small as a means of placating the now less than impressed Region Police Commander.

Quickly this new position gained publicity that far exceeded what was in reality a public servants position within the Premier's Department. Mike Carlton certainly thought so:

And as I've said, the big news in Sydney today is the Police Service and the sudden surprising move by 'our' Commander Clive Small, now to join the Premiers Department as a special adviser on Crime announced today. It's being hailed all around, as I said, a smart political and policing strategy that underlines the Government's commitment to fighting crime and so and so on. But is it all that it seems?

Note the change in Carlton's attitude towards the Government's 'commitment' to fighting crime in the space of just six or seven months. Carlton had caned the Carr Government's handling of crime and Cabramatta in the wake of the Cabramatta Inquiry report.

Carlton's support for Clive Small surfaced in an interview with Michael Costa, the NSW Police Minister, in fact in the very first question.

> *Carlton: Why has Clive Small moved to the Premier's Department?*
>
> *Costa: Well as I've said from day one when I became Minister that I'd like to see a greater coordination of government activities...*
>
> *Carlton: But on Friday, you wanted Clive Small sacked.*
>
> *Costa: Who?*
>
> *Carlton: I'll repeat that. On Friday you wanted Clive Small sacked.*
>
> *Costa: That's complete nonsense. Mike, absolute complete nonsense. I don't know who told you that but it's complete nonsense.*
>
> *Carlton: I have it on a totally reliable source that you had a blazing row on Friday with the Police Commissioner and demanded Clive Small be sacked along with three or four other Police Officers who you no longer wanted in the service.*

My experience when working for Costa was that his high level meetings usually involved just him and his highly regarded adviser Mark Greenhill and when it involved meeting Ryan it usually included Ryan's Chief of Staff, Bernie Aust. Certainly neither Costa nor Greenhill ever leaked confidential conversations of meetings in my experience and neither did Bernie Aust. So who would have told Carlton of this 'alleged' blazing row? Whoever it was, Carlton persisted, with the questioning.

Carlton: There is every point in pursuing it because my source is...utterly reliable. I want you to think very carefully before you answer it, do you deny that you demanded, asked, requested or ordered Peter Ryan to sack Clive Small. Now you think carefully before you answer it.

Costa:...whoever said that to you is misleading you completely, Mike and I suggest that I'm not going to continue that line of conversation...

And then:

Carlton: I am also reliably told that you referred to Clive Small as a self promoter who you wanted out.

Costa: I don't know who's told you all of that, Mike, but your being mislead. Severely...If you weren't in the room or you weren't in the situation where I was having the conversation, why are you repeating one part of the conversation and claiming that it's fact...

Carlton: Because I know...

Carlton: Why move him out of the Police Service?

Costa: Because HE indicated to my staff that he was interested in a change, I thought it was a good idea...He's not a special adviser to the Premier. He is a public servant or performing the functions of a public servant.

Clive Small was never a 'special advisor' to the Premier. He was filling the role of a public servant on secondment from the NSW Police. Carlton continued:

> *Thanks very much indeed. Michael Costa, the Police Minister. I'm not being misled. I have this story, I have this version of events on good reliable sources and I stand by that. I have said absolutely, one hundred per cent. That Clive Small has been moved sideways after a furious row between Michael Costa and Peter Ryan in which Costa demanded that Clive Small be sacked. This is a face saver, a patch up job, to paper over what is becoming a widening chasm between the Police Minister and his Commissioner and I don't resile from a word of it.*

The only problem with all of the above is that there never was a 'blazing row' between Costa and Ryan. Peter Ryan was a non-confrontationalist, he was a British-style negotiator, he was not the robust, aggressive Aussie like Costa. My experience in that time was that Costa did a lot of the talking and Ryan did lot of the listening, but there were no 'blazing rows'.

On 28 May 2002, after Ken Moroney was appointed Police Commissioner, Carlton commented on the appointment on the radio:

> *...but the government's passed up the man who's arguably the best and brightest cop in the state, the assistant commissioner Clive Small, he did apply for the job but plainly he was never going to get it. I think it's a shame. Clive Small is the sharpest crime fighter in the police*

service, the detective that led the hunt for Ivan Milat, the
commander who turned around Cabramatta. I think it's a
pity his talents aren't being used in the top job...

It appeared to me that Carlton suddenly knew a lot about the
NSW Police. Where did he get all this information about Clive
Small from?

> *Carlton: Why didn't Clive Small get the job?*
> *Costa: Well look I really don't want to focus on the process,*
> *it's been completed, there was an independent panel that*
> *had a look at this.*
> *Carlton: Oh come on, they all work for the government.*
> *They're not independent.*
> *Costa: Well they're independent of me. And the decision*
> *was made and endorsed this morning at Cabinet that Ken*
> *Moroney should be the next Commissioner.*

In the media barrage across the radio waves, I went from hero
to zero. From the hero of Cabramatta (which I never was) to
a 'so called whistleblower', to a 'fake Detective Sergeant', a
'discredited ex plod', and a right wing drongo. For example:

> *Meanwhile the Redfern riots and this Parliamentary*
> *Inquiry that's going on. I see that the right wing rabble,*
> *the right wing ratbags are now lining up to do their best to*
> *discredit this inquiry, to claim it's a sham, a cover up by*
> *the Carr Government...And of course the usual suspects in*
> *the media jumping up and down on their perches predicting*
> *doom and disaster and so on and so on. And of course that*

drongo Tim Priest, the so called whistleblower, is wheeled out again. Largely I think to keep pushing his ridiculous claim for hundreds of thousands of dollars of compensation from the Police. I think that's mainly what it's all about.

This city is going to be torn apart by gang warfare the likes of which we have never seen before, announced Tim Priest, in his apocalyptic lecture to the Quadrant magazine mafia back in 2003.

Commonly but wrongly billed as a former Detective Sergeant turned police whistleblower, Priest blows only his own trumpet. He has long been the pin up boy of the rat bag right, the rabble rousers who screech, almost daily, that a police force gutted by the Wood Royal Commission has surrendered the streets to murderous Lebanese Muslim terrorists plotting to slaughter us all in our beds.

The *Quadrant* article was from my speech to the Quadrant society. I have looked over my 'apocalyptic' speech many times and I just can't see where I wrote that Lebanese Muslim terrorists were plotting to 'slaughter us in our beds'.

Carlton then predicted the future of Middle Eastern gangs which is very telling, particularly in relation to the reality that Sydney is facing now:

Yes, there are gangs of Lebanese criminals, just as there are Vietnamese drug rackets, just as Italian Mafioso once ruled the Sydney Markets. But the worst of them have been broken up, with their ringleaders behind bars.

In the *Sun Herald* on the 29 March 2009, veteran police reporter Les Kennedy wrote a groundbreaking article headlined 'The Rise and Rise of New Gangs'.

They call themselves the MBM—the Muslim Brotherhood Movement—a gang of 600 men who boast they are the toughest and best young street fighters of Middle Eastern descent in Sydney...The sudden appearance of MBM, with its growing membership recruited predominantly from the city's south western suburbs, has alarmed senior police already battling to combat open warfare among outlaw motorcycle gangs... it's emblem features two crossed pistols and a hand grenade and its leadership remains unclear to officers of both the Organised Crime and Gang Squad and Middle Eastern Organised Crime Squad.

Police say a fortnight ago MBM members embarked upon a campaign of random assaults on men who crossed the path of the mob of about 100 toughs stalking Darlinghurst and Kings Cross during the Gay and Lesbian Mardi Gras.

The emergence of MBM also coincides with the rise of two other urban Sydney gangs—the Parra Boyz or Asesinoz MC and Brothers for Life or BFL. Police say BFL—with a logo featuring crossed machine-guns—is not dissimilar to MBM in its extremist views, but membership numbers are unknown.

Police describe Asesinoz, comprising teenagers of Middle Eastern decent, as 'tough kids' who use the video sharing website YouTube to promote Islamic extremism and anti-Australian actions such as flag burning.

Its creation follows that of the Notorious bikie gang, comprising members of Middle Eastern and Pacific Islander extraction...

These gangs did not just evolve overnight and the gang leaders that were behind bars, according to Carlton's sources, are obviously out and about or were never behind bars in the first place. One can only hope that Carlton's police sources are no longer in the NSW police and if they are, they do not have a position of influence within current gang squad operations.

One of the key features of the phenomenal crime problems amongst Middle Eastern and North African youth in southwest Paris in the 1990s was the role of certain 'left wing' media personalities. These pundits played down the growing crime problems and talked down journalists, police and other community leaders, who were attempting to get the message out about the rising trend of anti social and criminal activities of some Muslim youths in Paris.

In my speech to *Quadrant* in 2003 on the Rise of Middle Eastern Crime in Australia, I cited an incident in Paris where 1,000 heavily armed French police, some in armoured vehicles, descended on a southwestern Paris suburb to arrest three offenders. I asked the obvious question: was the sheer numbers of police on the raid connected to a serious terrorist threat? That would have been the obvious scenario to most readers. No it wasn't. The police were there to arrest three Muslim youths for a number of criminal offences and the sheer number of police was a safety issue as the suburbs the police were entering often resulted in spontaneous rioting at the sight of police arresting young residents in their neighbourhood.

These scenes, according to the French media, are not uncommon. The later Paris riots that brought the country to a standstill revolved around Middle Eastern and north African French immigrants who defy the police and challenge the state in a violent and provocative manner. The article by Theodore Dalrymple called 'Barbarians at the gates of Paris' is an interesting exploration of the issues surrounding the French experience with Middle Eastern-related crime.

In NSW there are similar less newsworthy instances that occur regularly when police in Middle Eastern-dominated suburbs make arrests. There are numerous reported incidents of police being surrounded by large groups of angry youths when they simply are imposing the rule of law.

Equally so are the problems confronting emergency wards in public hospitals where often violent relatives and friends disregard hospital rules that most citizens obey without question and attempt to impose their own standards on medical staff. They are nearly always of Middle Eastern descent. Why?

The Cronulla riots showed exactly what a small element of the Middle Eastern community is capable of when 'fired up'. Whether we reach the levels of violence that Paris has endured remains to be seen. Certainly some of the youths that live in these poorer parts of Paris have had a hard road since emigrating to France, but there are considerable numbers of youths that live in these areas that are habitual criminals and they should be treated as such, not pandered to and excused by academics who cry 'marginalised' as a defence to what is often unprovoked and unacceptable behavior. If we continue to listen and be influenced by this attitude we will most certainly head down the same path as France and other European countries.

The choice is ours.

The fact that the current Premier of NSW, Nathan Rees, and his Attorney General John Hatzistergos, on behalf of a very, very concerned community, had to hastily enact unprecedented tough new anti-gang laws in 2009 is testament to Carlton's lack of real knowledge about crime in Sydney. He may be an expert on Sydney's northern beaches where he resides, but it is far from the reality of life for young and old alike around central Sydney, the southern, western and south-western suburbs, where it is a major concern to residents.

In my article in *Quadrant* in 2003, I warned about the trends of growing Middle Eastern crime and of inadequate policing of gangs in Sydney. I certainly did lay part of the blame on a police force that was gutted publicly by the Wood Royal Commission and left impotent as a result of some of their recommendations. I did say that Cronulla would be a battleground at some point with Middle Eastern youth because there were overwhelming reports of anti-social and intimidating behaviour by some Middle Eastern youths towards local residents.

What Carlton failed to outline was the complete lack of focus by the now discredited Crime Agencies Command from 1997 to 2001 to tackle Middle Eastern crime in any meaningful way. It took Police Commissioner Ken Moroney to set up Task Force Gain to look into the growing trends of violence, for example the drive-by shootings that had began in Cabramatta in the late 1990s and escalated in south-west Sydney with warring factions of Middle Eastern crime families.

Mike Carlton has taken aim on two prominent people after their death—for example his attack on Stan Zemanek after he had died and his attack on the high profile and controversial civil libertarian, and former member of the Police Board, John Marsden after he died brought significant public outrage for attacking subjects no longer able to defend themselves. His attack on Stan Zemanek happened to be the very day Stan was being laid to rest.

I too have come under his fire. Take for example when Carlton wrote wrongly in the *Sydney Morning Herald* that I was a 'disgruntled junior copper under Deborah Wallace's command'. I was never 'under' Deborah Wallace's command. We had worked together as Detective Sergeants at Cabramatta in April 1997. Deborah Wallace was actually on rotation to a uniform supervisor's job within Cabramatta Police Station at the time, albeit for a very short time. Wallace later went to Internal Affairs as a Section 66 Inspector. Absolutely nothing to do with Cabramatta. She later returned to Cabramatta after I had been transferred out of the Police Station, following the 'rebellion'. So the notion that I had worked 'under' Wallace' was just misinformation.

In Deborah Wallace's interview with Peter Bodor QC on 14 June 2003 at page 20, she says on two separate occasions:

> *I did not work with Tim Priest, maybe for just a short time in 1997 and certainly never worked operation(ly) with Tim Priest.*

The way I interpreted the articles, as did others, is that I must have resented working under a female who was apparently senior in rank.

There was also a series of three *Herald* articles by former journalist Stephen Gibbs published in 2006 for which I sued the *Sydney Morning Herald* and the matter was settled out of court. That defamation never even reached the 'imputations' stage, so wrong was the information.

I was also supposedly the new CEO of the Police Citizens Youth Club organization, according to Mike Carlton. Yes I had an office at the Redfern PCYC. I had become an adviser to the NSW Police Ministry on the merits of the revolutionary American police anti gang program DARE. Sadly, the NSW Education Department, in particular, a few backward thinking high school principals, were violently opposed to any discussion on this award winning program, that breaks the nexus between school kids, gangs and drugs. How well we could have done with DARE in south western Sydney over the past decade.

Be that as it may, it didn't mean I was about to embark on a 'takeover' of the entire PCYC structure.

I jokingly asked Carlton to meet me at the Cabramatta PCYC for a quick punch up and then maybe a chat afterwards about the real state of the streets in Cabramatta. Alas, Mike declined and instead, 'wrote me up' in the following Saturday's *Herald*. He must have been short of content that week I can only assume.

This article in the *Herald* on 31 May 2002 shows a journalist who is out of touch with their topic. Cabramatta still seems to be a focus of media and police relations, where each is desperate to erase the past and paint a positive picture, despite the reality on the ground. This article was headlined: 'Lunching in the mean streets with life and limb intact.'

Contrary to what we have been told, the streets of downtown Cabramatta are not thronged with gun toting gangsters, the gutters running with blood and littered with ammo clips.

Not last Saturday (May 26 2002) anyway. I went there for a look at the invitation of the local state Labor MP, Reba Meagher, about whom I fear I have been rather unkind in recent years. How disappointing not to be shot at nor once offered a smorgasbord of illegal chemicals. John Street, Cabramatta looked like any Sydney suburban shopping centre on a busy Saturday morning. Well, like any Saigon shopping centre, but that's not the point.

After not being gunned down by the 5-T gang, we lunched with the senior local coppers, Superintendent Frank Hansen and his crime manager, Detective Chief Inspector Debbie Wallace, an engaging pair who believe, convincingly, that the tide of crime has turned on their patch.

This view may have dimmed with the shooting of seven wedding guests later that very night, but the crime statistics do bear out their claim that Cabramatta is getting safer. Slowly but surely.

It's easy to lunch anywhere safely in the presence of two uniformed senior police. In their company in Cabramatta you will certainly not be offered a 'smorgasbord of chemicals'. You probably will not be shot at either.

Carlton would have barely finished his last crab leg and pork roll when a wedding party arrived to celebrate Cabramatta-style at a restaurant just metres from where Carlton, Frank Hansen and Wallace feasted.

I suppose Carlton was fortunate not to receive an invitation to the traditional Cabramatta wedding just a few hours later, right there in John Street Cabramatta. A total of seven people were shot, including a young boy. It was no ordinary wedding, in fact the brother of one of the biggest gangsters in Cabramatta was responsible for the shooting.

You have to smile at the irony of Mike Carlton venturing into Cabramatta to give the recently cleaned up suburb his seal of approval and as soon as he is heading safely back up the highway, a nearby restaurant celebrates a wedding, Cabramatta-style, with a shootout.

8.

SYDNEY CONFIDENTIAL

I know that 'freedom of the press' is a fundamental principle of democracy, but there must come a time when that freedom becomes abuse and there needs to be reparation—not just through the defamation courts.

There are a lot of journalists who are prepared to sell their souls for access to quick and easy headlines and they should be exposed publicly. Front-page headlines that come from 'sources' known only to a journalist usually come at a price, and that price is usually an IOU in the form of a future article in favour of that informant.

The use of the media by the Wood Royal Commission is well documented and mentioned at length in previous chapters. The final report by Justice Wood in 1997 even contained a tribute to the role of the media during the corruption hearings. I still find it disturbing that no one from the media, with the exception of Steve Barratt, took an interest in the story of Task

Force Bax. There were a few journalists in the hearing rooms on the day that Justice Wood and John Agius spoke of the overdose 'emergency' in Kings Cross in July 1996. Those same journalists were probably present when KX15 was 'uncovered' as a Commission agent against Peter Kay and Bill Bayeh. Yet it appears to me that none of them connected the dots to the *60 Minutes* program *Dirty Work* produced by Steve Barratt in 2003 and the matters were allowed to rest without a hint of so called investigative journalism.

Why? Why didn't any journalists probe such a vital and controversial story? Were the alliances between the media and the WRC so strong?

The links between the media, the Wood Royal Commission and the police in the Peter Ryan era were strong. I have no doubt they remain so today. In that sense, certain sections of the media have played a significant role in the progress of law enforcement in NSW in the past 15 years—far more so than they are entitled too. Many journalists are far from independent and a few of them in the past wielded enormous power both within the media itself, the Government and ultimately within the NSW Police.

This behaviour is never more evident than within the ranks of crime reporters from various newspapers.

A popular hotel in Surry Hills used to be a favourite meeting place for journos and police in the past. On a Friday night, the hotel filled with young and old journalists and a few senior police, all detectives. The senior detectives, over a few beers, would divulge what major police operations were in progress and a few that were planned. The journalists were given a heads up on just what operations were about to be finalized so that they could report on them, on the front page usually, virtually as the arrests were being made.

This relationship kept the editors of the large newspapers happy and the journalists themselves had to do little or no leg work other than write up the article, usually from a police fact sheet or a report.

The senior police were very happy as they managed to get their names on the front page and became somewhat of a 'legend' in the eyes of an unsuspecting public who could be forgiven for thinking that these senior police were the only detectives working in the state.

Police media worked in much the same fashion. The Police Media Unit was highly successful in giving the impression that all was well in the NSW Police and that crime was being driven down across the state, when in reality the streets had become far less safe and drug dealing in particular was totally out of control.

It was interesting to learn how some senior police forged strong links with certain journalists and even more interesting to see which journalists were aligned with certain senior police.

There is nothing illegal about this practice until confidential and sensitive police documents begin to find their way into the hands of the media. If those documents disclose a need for the public to be warned of a danger or an emerging crime trend, then that is the role of a journalist to seek out the truth and report on it. But when those documents are leaked to discredit individual police officers or leaked to help with an individual's promotion prospects, then it is a form of corruption. The amount of confidential and 'sensitive documents' that were leaked during the Peter Ryan years 1996-2002 were simply astonishing and little was done about it by the so called media watchdogs in NSW.

This is in stark contrast to years gone past where a detective's reputation was usually enhanced by the quality of his arrests and convictions, not by his media contacts.

I do not believe it was accidental that the rise and rise of media 'spin doctors' in Sydney coincided with arrival of the Bob Carr-led ALP Government in NSW in 1999. Bob Carr was a former journalist and an ardent follower of American history. It is no secret that the USA is the home of media spin going back at least to the days of the Vietnam war.

The NSW Government employed a legion of media types whose job was to put out good news stories for the government and hose down the bad ones. Indeed it was a well known fact around town that the Government had media staff working the night shift to prepare daily briefings for the Government on what had occurred in NSW overnight. It was a brilliant and effective tactic that kept the Carr Government mostly on the front foot when controversial issues arose and the Government needed to respond to media enquiries almost immediately.

Bob Carr announced he would be 'tough on crime' when he became Premier. As part of that, the NSW Police were important contributors to his strategy and so followed a daily flow of 'good' news stories about the new Police Commissioner Peter Ryan and how he was turning things around in NSW following the 'shocking' revelations of the Wood Royal Commission into police corruption. So good was that media management of Ryan that it took nearly five years for the cracks to begin showing in his failed policing strategies, despite the obvious signs of decay in and around Sydney, especially in Cabramatta.

Morgan Ogg was one of the first Sydney journalists to see through the Ryan veil. Ogg wrote a number of articles critical of Ryan and his regime in its early days, which made him particularly unpopular with sections of the NSW Police and the Carr Government's spin machine.

One senior police officer that was regularly reported on in the Fairfax Press was Clive Small.

Clive Small came to prominence following the Harry Blackburn 'fiasco'. Harry Blackburn was a former Police Superintendent who was wrongly accused of serious sex crimes. He was subsequently cleared of the charges through a police re-investigation of the crimes, conducted by Clive Small. A Royal Commission was set up and became known as the Blackburn Royal Commission.

Small was hallmarked as someone to watch from then on, and was particularly supported by journalist Neil Mercer:

Flashback, 1982. Two NSW Detectives and two reporters are tucking into lunch at Fishwives restaurant in Surry Hills. As the conversation flows, the senior officer leans over to one of the journalists and, indicating his colleague, Detective Sergeant Clive Small, says, 'You want to keep an eye on him, he's going to be Commissioner one day'.

Neil Mercer would subsequently report regularly on the backpacker murders in the 1990s, where Clive Small was the Officer in Charge and he would later write a book on the investigation and conviction of one of the suspects, Ivan Milat.

It is interesting to track the rise of Clive Small through the opinions of the media that reported on him. Alex Mitchell wrote an article in 1997 for the *Herald* titled, 'From the ashes of the CIB, A Detective Force is resurrected'.

> *The Criminal Investigation Bureau, axed in 1987 by then Police Chief John Avery, is being revived by Police Commissioner Peter Ryan.*
>
> *The officer in charge of the new force of detectives will be Clive Small, who headed the team which caught and successfully prosecuted serial killer Ivan Milat. He will be promoted from Superintendent to Assistant Commissioner to head a plain clothes empire.*
>
> *Mr. Small's 'dramatic' rise in the police hierarchy ends years of virtual isolation during Commissioner Tony Lauer's reign when he was twice overlooked for promotion.*

Alex Mitchell's exclusive on the 17 June 2001, had me scratching my head:

> *The Upper House inquiry into Cabramatta's policing tested the credibility and often the patience of all ranks of the NSW Police Service.*
>
> *Sergeant Priest has been cast as a loose cannon. But his whistle blowing had the effect of galvanizing the police and the Carr Government into remedial action.*
>
> *If he had made such public criticisms before the existence of the Wood Royal Commission, he almost certainly would have lost his career in the police force.*
>
> *In the bad old days officers who went public with their concerns about police procedures or rigged crime statistics were given short shrift.*

It is to their great credit that senior police, harshly criticized by this rebellious junior officer, have handled his catalogue of complaints with such maturity and professionalism.

A week later Alex Mitchell wrote this:

Cabramatta flourished as Australia's drugs capital because front line police were demoralized, frustrated and mismanaged, according to a report by State MPs to be released next month.

Drug related crimes ran out of control while the Police Service instructed local officers on keeping crime statistics and introducing new management practices.

MPs were horrified by the warfare between senior and junior officers over the true state of the suburbs shocking crime wave and angered by the buck-passing.

Although the 100 page report is strictly confidential until tabled in Parliament, the Sun Herald understands its preliminary draft is scathing about past police management at Cabramatta but optimistic about reforms announced in March by Premier Bob Carr and now in the hands of Assistant Commissioner Clive Small, the State's most experienced operational policeman.

Alex Mitchell didn't quite get the last sentence right. An operational policeman, is one that carries a gun and handcuffs and makes arrests on a fairly regular basis. He is usually on the roster at a suburban police station or a squad and carries out duties such as arresting, interviewing and charging suspects, or involved in duties that regularly put him or her into contact with the public.

Clive Small was an administrator in charge of a police region at that time, not an operational policeman. As far as experienced went, I would have thought Mal Brammer, the head of Police Internal Affairs at the time, was easily the most experienced detective in the state, given his long record of front line policing prior to becoming a senior commissioned officer. But it was Clive Small who appeared to be being groomed by politicians and the media for a promising future.

My own so-called 'catalogue of complaints' must have been reasonably close to the mark as Alex reports 'drug related crime ran out of control' and 'Cabramatta flourished as Australia's drug capital'. I think my complaints may have been 'justified'.

The Cabramatta Inquiry was not the only inquiry Small was to face in the next few years. He, along with the NSW Police hierarchy, would face the Police Integrity Commission over the 'failed reform process' after the Wood Royal Commission.

Some members of the Police Reform Unit tried to bring about reform in line with the recommendations of the Wood Royal Commission. They were shabbily treated by the NSW Police and the final report on the entire process by the Police Integrity Commission came under heavy criticism for basically reporting, nothing. Neil Mercer:

The police hierarchy whose inner workings were placed under the microscope is long gone.

The Police Integrity Commission has done itself no favours with a long and expensive inquiry that has resulted in a report recommending, well nothing.

The PIC report did contain one extraordinary passage in relation to Clive Small that was recorded in the notes belonging to the head of the Reform Unit, Superintendent Ken Seddon.

The PIC Operation Malta Report at 7.53:

Seddon's notes for 19 October 2000 record that at about 5pm Darren Goodsir, a journalist, rang him and told him Ritchie was going to hold a press conference the following day and that Goodsir was offering to help. According to Seddon's notes, Goodsir said that he knew about Seddon being under investigation and asked what is was for. Seddon responded that he did not know. Goodsir said that he would put a call into Small and ask what it was about.

About 15 minutes later, Goodsir rang Seddon and said that Small had told him:

"All about what I (Seddon) was being investigated for. It was for 'rorting' travel claims and submitting fraudulent tax claims. Asked for a comment. I declined."

According to Seddon's notes Small phoned him at 6.00pm that same day. He told Seddon that Goodsir had rung him and there was going to be a huge article in the Sydney Morning Herald the following day. Small said that he told Goodsir that he had no comment on the subject.

Seddon's notes record that about 9.00pm that same day, 19 October 2000, Small telephone Seddon again and advised him that Ritchie had put out a press release. In the conversation, as recorded by Seddon, Small said:

In the article he (Ritchie) talks about having had a meeting with Ken Moroney to discuss how he can deal with; and these are my notes—The corrosive nature of the competitiveness of the senior executives from Crime Agencies and Internal Affairs who are obsessed with their own egos (my words not Small's) Is that me he's talking about?

To which Seddon said, 'I would say so, yes'. According to Seddon, Small then said: Well mate that just confirms everything everybody always said about him being malicious and untrustworthy. I don't know. I've finished with him now. All I've ever done for him was to look after his interests but I'll tell you mate I'm stuffed if I know what to do.'

Seddon's notes record him responding that Ritchie would just have to get by without Small's help. Small advised Seddon that Ritchie was holding a press conference the next day.

The PIC didn't appear to be overly concerned about the conversation between a senior NSW Police Officer, a journalist and Ken Seddon, other than to report the occurrence in their final analysis.

Neil Mercer also reported on the disappointment of Clive Small in being overlooked for the position of Deputy Police Commissioner:

For Commander Clive Small, 55, it was another disappointment in an extraordinary career that had seen him rise to be the State's most senior and respected detective. It was Small who won national and international recognition leading the team that arrested backpacker killer Ivan Milat. He has also investigated the collapse of the Nugan Hand Merchant Bank (with Jack Whelan), been praised by a Royal Commission for controversially clearing Harry Blackburn (wrongly accused of rape) and written a groundbreaking report on the nature of organized crime.

After 37 years, he was a top cop, but with Costa's announcement of the two young deputy commissioners, his ambition to make it all the way appeared at an end.

There was speculation that he would quit, a prospect that would have been welcomed by broadcaster Alan Jones, who has been intensely critical of Small.

But the idea alarmed several people in the Carr Government. Heading for an election with crime as a major issue, the last thing they wanted was for such a high profile police officer with an unmatched record as an investigator and trouble shooter to jump ship. Within days, a staff member from Carr's office told Small not to do anything hasty.

The reality of the Premier's Department position is that it was a public servant's position. When the Commissioner's job finally became vacant after Peter Ryan resigned in 2002, Small threw his hat into the ring and Neil Mercer and Stephen Gibbs reported on it in the *Herald*.

The State's most celebrated detective, Commander Clive Small, has thrown his hat into the ring for the job he has coveted for the best part of his 36 years of service, NSW Police Commissioner.

Now Clive Small was the state's 'most celebrated' detective'. In September 2003 it was Stephen Gibbs's turn to write up the career of Clive Small, firstly on the apparent victory in Cabramatta in just 12 months:

DRUG CAPITAL LOSES ITS CROWN.

Cabramatta is no longer the drug capital of Australia, or even NSW, the officer in charge of the region said yesterday.

Commander Clive Small said that when he had taken control of the Greater Hume region early this year he faced problems on the streets between police and the community and in the Cabramatta Police Station itself.

Drastic action had to be taken "and the results spoke for themselves". The feedback we are getting is Cabramatta is nothing like it was 12 months ago. I do not believe you can any longer describe Cabramatta as the drug capital of Australia or the drug capital of NSW, he said.

He said the successes in Cabramatta did not mean the drug problem had spread elsewhere. Police had identified about 60 drug houses in Cabramatta in January but now there were only one or two.

Cabramatta had not lost its crown as a drug capital and more importantly, the problems did spread elsewhere. If you live in Liverpool, which is a stone's throw from Cabramatta, you would agree.

To suggest that the drugs, the addicts and the gangs, just shut up shop and disappeared is puzzling. They had to go somewhere and there has been ample television coverage over the years of rampant drug dealing in the main street of Liverpool as well as a rise in street violence particularly around Westfield and the adjoining plaza and the odd murder or two involving Middle Eastern and Asian youths.

The 'good news' stories about Cabramatta continued over the next few years. One article appeared just prior to the last

NSW election in 2006 when the ALP Government was looking a bit shaky and the very safe seat of Cabramatta was looking even shakier.

An article in the *Herald* weekend edition on the 7-8 October, 2006 by journalist Emily Dunn started with a quick culinary description of Cabramatta with the overwhelming aroma of freshly baked bread, the scent of basil wafting from the noodle houses and the stench of the fishmongers near the Woolworths Supermarket. There were descriptions of elderly Vietnamese playing mah-jong over a steaming bowl of noodles in Freedom Plaza.

Ms Dunn reported on stories from locals including a Barbara Crawford, who from her stool at the Cabramatta Inn said that things are better nowadays, especially the decline in comatose drug addicts littering the streets. The article quotes police reports of 74 heroin overdoses per month in 2000, dropping to just 15 a month by 2002.

A curious statistic was given by the then Cabramatta Crime Manager to the journalist stating that narcotic possession detected by police was 1200 in 1998-99 but went down to 128 in the current period. That is a remarkable drop, unprecedented almost.

No longer were locals tripping over unconscious heroin addicts, avoiding drug dealers and having their shops ransacked by crazed druggies.

The article ends with more culinary treasures such as barbecued meats hanging in the windows, whilst bric-a-bac shops spilled onto lanes and footpaths.

Coming up to an election, Cabramatta had not only lost its 'drug capital' claim, but now looked as though it was an almost crime-free 'Asian metropolis'. But was it?

Coincidentally an article by the *Herald's* sister paper, the *Sun-Herald* the day after Emily Dunne's piece, gave a rather different picture. In fact the underlying heroin and organized crime problems were not quite finished in Cabramatta.

The article by Louise Hall and AAP on 8 October 2006 had a headline: 'Court told of $93m laundering operation'.

It reported that raids by the Australian Crime Commission closed down a major money laundering operation. No less than $93 million dollars in cash had been transferred out of Australia to various parts of Asia from four money transaction businesses in Cabramatta, as well as in Bankstown and Melbourne. All those involved were Vietnamese-born and most resided or operated businesses within Cabramatta, Bankstown or in Melbourne. In addition, a man named Van Loi Nguyen was charged with trafficking a commercial quantity of heroin, around 1.5 kilograms. The operation had been sending the cash proceeds of drug sales through international money transfer offices, one of which was located within the My Le Hoa fashion shop in Cabramatta.

The amount of money laundered and sent from Australia was staggering. Despite the so called heroin drought and NSW Police crackdown on drugs and gangs in Cabramatta, $93 million still managed to be collected, laundered and sent overseas.

I have no doubt that Cabramatta looks and feels different to what it did when I was there in the 1990s. To make wild claims that the suburb has lost its status as an organized crime hot spot is both foolish and dishonest.

It's what the ALP Government in NSW and their political police force have become widely recognized for—first rate spin and the appearance of change without the reality.

When the Redfern riots erupted one Sunday night and continued into the early hours of Monday, Neil Mercer was back on board to report that the former 'Assistant Commissioner' Clive Small had warned the Government in September 2002 of its possibility:

> *The Carr Government and Senior Police ignored, or reacted weakly to, repeated warnings that Redfern's heroin trade was out of control, the Sunday Telegraph has been told.*
>
> *The NSW Government was first warned of the heroin problems in September 2002 by the Premier's own adviser on Crime, former Assistant Commissioner Clive Small.*
>
> *In November 2003 three months before the latest riot, Mr. Small again warned the Government, including the office of Police Minister John Watkins, but was told everything in Redfern was all right.*

The truth about Redfern is that it has been a festering mess for decades with action only being taken every time there is a riot, in this case, following the tragic death of TJ Hickey. I worked in Redfern in the early 1990s and saw the hopelessness of people living in squalor within the backdrop of Australia's premier city. I took newly-minted Police Minister Michael Costa for a walk through the 'slums' to show him the situation in January 2002. The walk through was covered by Quentin Dempster on the ABC's *Stateline* program. What Clive Small was saying was nothing new.

The closeness of media and police which ventures into

incompetence was evidenced by a *Four Corners* program made by Chris Masters on the 'backpacker murders' before any arrests were made.

Clive Small was interviewed by Masters for *Four Corners* and the names MILAT/EVEREST were clearly visible on a board behind him as he was interviewed by Masters. It appears that the names meant nothing to either of them, as a subsequent 'preview' tape was cleared by Small and the broadcast took place a few days later.

A member of the Milat family rang *Four Corners* and Task Force Air shortly after it screened. How fortunate it was that Ivan Milat and the members of his family, despite seeing their name on the whiteboard within the Task Force AIR office and then ringing police to complain about it, did not bother to get rid of incriminating evidence immediately that they became aware that they were suspects.

There are those associated with the Milat brief that still believe there was most certainly a second offender. Where is that offender now? And who is investigating that possibility?

The evidence from renowned ballistics expert, Gerard Dutton from the Tasmanian Police and a former NSW Detective, was critical in Milat's conviction. He did work on the Task Force and was interviewed on Crime Investigation Australia on Foxtel over the Milat story.

He is a very highly regarded police expert, who was in no doubt that a second offender was with Milat during at least some of the murders, contrary to Small's continued line that Milat alone was responsible. Justice Hunt, who sat through the lengthy trial of Milat, also made special mention of a second offender as having been involved.

Gerard Dutton said that in his long experience in investigating murders, over 20 years in fact, that a second offender was involved. He gave compelling ballistic reasons on the evidence found during the enquiry as to why he believed that.

Clive Small was the head of the Task Force, not the arresting and charging detective. Quite often through media articles and crime shows he is portrayed as the man that appears most responsible for Milat's arrest and conviction.

In this case, the dozens of dedicated detectives and uniformed police who made up Task Force AIR, actually solved the Milat case.

9.

THE STARK REALITY OF POLICING IN NEW SOUTH WALES

The NSW Police Force that I joined decades ago bears no resemblance to the institution we now have in 2009. There are a number of people that will say that is a good thing, in some instances they may be right. However, many of the 'successful' elements of the old NSW Police did not need changing and what we are now seeing is the result of ill-informed and ill-conceived changes.

The specialisation aspect is still to be perfected and it needs to be, urgently. The disasters of the Crime Agencies investigative model under Peter Ryan has left massive problems in crime intelligence-gathering in particular, which is the lifeblood of a competent and capable modern police force.

Many of the serious crimes that have flourished in NSW in the past decade have been the result of a lack of specialised response by NSW Police towards specific criminal activities. The indifferent attitude to Middle Eastern crime by Crime Agencies has, I believe, been mostly responsible for the dramatic rise in organised crime in this city in the past decade.

The blowing up of ATMs across Sydney in the past 12 months is a prime example of a police force not being on the ball and anticipating likely crime trends that could effect this city. The ATM epidemic appears unstoppable. It will be just a matter of when and not if, one of these ATM explosions kills an innocent bystander or causes a catastrophic building collapse.

The ATM robberies trend has been around for at least two or three years in Europe, often with the same ethnicity amongst the offenders involved there as it is here. What are the other trends evident in Europe, including the United Kingdom, that we should be aware of and indeed anticipating? Is there a NSW Crime Intelligence unit that actively seeks out this intelligence from overseas and actually begins monitoring these trends as they occur and not a few months later when the media begin to report on the incidents?

When the NSW Police Force had the highly productive and successful Bureau of Crime Intelligence (BCI) there was little that occurred in NSW that this group did not know about. They actively investigated emerging crime trends, and were among the first police forces in this country to track the rise of the Italian organized crime groups of the 1970s and 1980s.

NSW Police needs to reinstate Target Development Teams that can work on emerging crime trends as they first appear and gather vital intelligence at the earliest possible moment. By doing this, they will get a window of opportunity to see who is behind the new trends before the problem grows too quickly and becomes unmanageable.

In 2003, I gave a speech to members of the Quadrant society on the rise of Middle Eastern crime in this country. The speech was later reprinted in *The Australian* newspaper and attracted considerable comment and media exposure. It also attracted critics that I did not know I had. Most of those critics played down the problem of Middle Eastern crime, and in some cases argued that it did not exist.

It is interesting to read the media releases and articles that are printed in defence of the Middle Eastern community by so called informed sources. One particular article caught my eye and it is a good example of just how little some people know about the subject they are writing about.

The article was headlined 'The myth of ethnic crime' and was compiled by a Sarah Stephen, in the *Green Left weekly news*. This one was dated 4 February 2004.

> *...There are suburbs in Sydney's west that have become synonymous with 'ethnic crime', thanks to a systematic campaign of hysteria by the corporate media in the past six years. Cabramatta is synonymous with 'Vietnamese triads' and Bankstown is synonymous with 'Lebanese gangs'.*

For a start, I don't think there has ever been a 'Vietnamese triad'. I have never seen them referred to as that. Triads, I understand, are a Chinese-based criminal group or 'Tong'. Triads were mostly Hong Kong and Macau-based but have spread to other parts of the globe, but I certainly never saw or heard of

'Vietnamese triads' in Cabramatta or indeed in Sydney. There were gangs most certainly, but not Vietnamese 'triads'.

This next paragraph astonished me:

> *Based on a handful of crimes committed in the Bankstown area in the past 6 years, including the stabbing death of 14 year old Edward Lee, the drive by shooting of the Lakemba police station, and the gang raping of a number of young women by a group young Lebanese Australians, the corporate media has run a sensationalist campaign about a 'crime wave' in south-western Sydney involving Lebanese gangs.*

Based on a 'handful' of crimes in the past six years? One of the criminals involved in the Lakemba Police Station shooting fled to Lebanon where he was arrested in connection with terrorism charges. He is now behind bars in NSW. The group also included the infamous murderer Michael Kanaan, now serving a life sentence in the Supermax section of Goulburn Prison for the murders of two young footballers in inner Sydney in July 1998.

The point I make is that playing down crime reports in an area that is predominantly Middle Eastern is not in anyone's interests, especially the Middle Eastern people who live in the area and who are predominantly law abiding, decent and hard working Australians. The area, like some other suburbs across Sydney, has some significant gang problems that will not go away simply because of misinformed and inaccurate press releases.

Reporting on ethnic based crime is a sensitive issue. When that crime represents a clear and present danger to all of our community, then it must be reported accurately. There is always the possibility that reporting those problems can inflame racist agendas and racist perceptions amongst small sections of the larger community.

I have first-hand knowledge of the problems that racial stereotyping can cause innocent individuals. My children have a variety of friends from several ethnic backgrounds, including Middle Eastern born and Australian raised kids. They are all typical young Aussies and are respectful, kind and generous but they encounter from time to time the fallout from less respectful Middle Eastern youth that have caused considerable problems across Sydney with violence and drug dealing.

Frequently these kids will be prevented from entering nightclubs because of their Middle Eastern appearance, usually because the security staff have had long and consistent problems with Middle Eastern thugs. Critically, most of these security staff are not Caucasian security guards but are indeed either Pacific Islander or Middle Eastern born.

It is hard to explain to these kids that it is not their fault nor is it an attitude representative of most Australians to preclude them from entertainment venues. But there is and has been a significant problem with Middle Eastern criminals causing trouble around entertainment premises. The city and eastern suburbs are prime examples.

The reasons for the outbreak of Middle Eastern crime are complex. It also appears to be a global problem, with similar incidences in France, Germany, Sweden, Holland, Denmark and the United Kingdom. All of those countries have significant Middle Eastern immigrant populations.

Marginalization and racism are often listed as an excuse for the over representation of Middle Eastern youth involved in crime. There would appear to have been some truth in that in previous generations. But what we are seeing now is second generation even third generation involvement in criminal activity and the argument I believe about marginalization being a factor holds little relevance.

I also see the problems of selective and weak policing as being a contributor to the almost disregard some Middle Eastern youth hold for authorities such as the police. At the end of the day, the rule of law has to be enforced and obeyed. That is how society maintains order and allows the average citizen to live in peace. When the rule of law breaks down, the machine breaks down and we are left with little else but an ungovernable society.

Selective policing took place under Peter Ryan and the Carr Government during the late 1990s and the earlier part of this decade. Senior police in NSW intentionally backed down to 'cultural and political pressure' and did not, in certain parts of southwest Sydney, enforce the rule of law as it is done in most other parts of the state.

Frightened of violent confrontation from large mobs of aggressive Middle Eastern youth, police were instructed to retreat in many instances and attempt to identify the offenders later and summons them to Court. This was standard practice and there are volumes of police incident reports that spell out that methodology. It was a cowardly form of policing and taught these gangsters that they need not fear the NSW Police. I mentioned in my speech to Quadrant that this in fact 'handed the keys of the city' to these marauding gangs to do as they please and in some instances, such as with the aftermath of the

Cronulla riots, that is exactly what they did.

The aftermath of the Cronulla riots was probably the darkest day in NSW Policing. Here we had a police force totally paralyzed by fear and incompetence, unable to protect the community it had sworn an oath to serve. Had the NSW Police taken action earlier in the day and dispersed the crowds of drunken young Caucasian men chanting 'Aussie, Aussie, Aussie', then the fallout may have been different. But these Caucasian youths did not just assemble one Sunday morning and start a riot. There were a number of incidents that provoked these young men to protest about violent acts against them by youths of Middle Eastern descent and the police should have taken action sooner, despite one senior NSW Police Officer trying to tell a shocked media group that there had only been 'one or two' reports of assaults against locals by Middle Eastern youths.

That begs a question: how reliable are the police statistics on Middle Eastern crime? I don't believe for one second that they reflect the true influence on crime that Middle Eastern youth have.

In 2009 the highly acclaimed Channel 7 series *Gangs of Oz* ran a program on Middle Eastern crime. It quoted Superintendent Ken McKay, a highly regarded detective, speaking about his experience as the head of the NSW Police Middle Eastern Crime Squad. He said: 'If they didn't invent it, they perfected it.'

Ken McKay was criticised for saying what he honestly thought.

What has really alarmed me over the past decade is the emergence of what I once described to a journalist as a 'perfect storm'. I was referring to the emergence of a new and even more worrying crime trend—the convergence of Middle Eastern criminals with Pacific Islander thugs and their associations with Outlaw Motorcycle Groups (OMCG). That is now a reality, with the recent bashing murder of a man at the Sydney Domestic Airport on 22 March 2009. At the time of writing this book, no one had been charged with the murder despite there being hundreds of people present and CCTV throughout the airport.

There are now a number of high profile OMCGs that have Middle Eastern members, including senior ranking ones. Janet Fife-Yeomans and Kara Lawrence wrote in the The Daily Telegraph on 6 May 2009 that Middle Eastern youth were becoming 'easy pickings' for recruitment into Outlaw Motorcycle Gangs and they quoted a Senior NSW Police Officer expressing his concern at the emergence of Muslim youth 'feeder' gangs.

This should be a massive wake up call to all Australian Police Forces and the Federal Government. There needs to be a National Law Enforcement effort to rid the country of this problem and it has to happen now, not two years down the track when the problem will be so entrenched it will be near impossible to deal with.

It is very interesting to see that traditional bikie gangs do not want a bar of the new Middle Eastern OMCGs as they violently disapprove of the focus they have brought upon the whole of the OMCG network.

The basic problem still remains a policing problem and unfortunately there is unlikely to be a massive change in the way we police in NSW that could go towards solving these urgent issues. Policing in NSW is more about appearance and media spin than it is about actually breaking the back of organized crime.

The *Sunday Telegraph's* editorial on the 7 June 2009 commenced with the heading: 'Get serious about gang warfare'.

> *Underworld violence is exploding across Sydney. Now it is time for the police and politicians to show the public who is in control.*
>
> *If Police Commissioner Andrew Scipione and Premier Nathan Rees are serious about getting a grip on gangs, drugs and organized crime, they must increase the scope and powers of the recently created Strike Force Raptor.*

Further on, the Editorial stated the obvious:

> *The same names keep arising in connection with apparent disparate activities. There are too many clear links for police and politicians to pretend any longer that any of this is coincidental.*

Is it too late to try and stem the tide of drive by shootings and rampant gang violence in this city? The disaster of the Crime Agencies model in NSW has condemned this city to the type of violence we will be seeing in the long term. It will not stop quickly and it definitely will not go away.

Despite the fact that Peter Ryan left as Police Commissioner nearly seven years ago his legacy lives on, tragically. His creation of Duty Officer is a British model that was never needed here and has caused major difficulties since it was introduced by

Ryan in the late 1990s. The position of Duty Officer is basically the same as the old Supervising Sergeant except the Supervising Sergeant of the past had probably at least 20 years' experience: some Duty Officers today have about half that. The old saying that 'you can't put an old head on young shoulders' is so true in policing.

When Ryan created these positions he increased the pay levels and Duty Officers were often earning $30,000 more than a Detective Sergeant with about five per cent of the Detective Sergeant's workload. It was unfair and I believe it was brought in to separate management from the cop on the street.

The Ryan-inspired promotion system was and is a disaster. The cost to the community for this position is about $50 million per year, year after year. It has helped drain the police budget and diverted funds that should have been used to fight crime. It has been more successful in developing an officer class mentality within the NSW Police and alienating the street cops from management. This flawed rank structure was visibly disastrous in Cabramatta back in 1999-2000 and it still is.

Experience in the NSW Police is no longer a major criteria for promotion with five to seven years' service now considered 'experienced'. In the past, experience was valuable, for example 15 years service was needed for promotion to Sergeant.

The next most crucial issue is that of police numbers. The NSW Police Force is appallingly undermanned. The automatic defence of any NSW Police Minister of the day when asked about police staffing levels is always: 'NSW has record police numbers'. They are right, if you had 25 extra cops this year than last year that is a record level. What they don't say is that in comparison to national and international standards, NSW police/civilian ratios are alarming.

For example: New York has 44,000 police at a ratio of 1 police officer to 200 civilians. The London Metropolitan Police have nearly 32,000 officers and their ratio is slightly higher. Both pale in comparison with New South Wales, where the ratio is 1 police pfficer to 440 civilians, double that of the NYPD.

How important are police numbers? They are critical in maintaining law and order and vital in controlling crime rates. Put simply, more cops mean safer streets. A glowing example is the rate of burglaries in New York which is around 287 per 100,000 population. In New South Wales we boast a massive 832 per 100,000 population. The figures are staggering and compelling.

The New South Wales Police Association wants an additional 3,000 cops. That is what they need right now—to bring our police strength up to the same ratio as the London Metropolitan Police would require an additional 8,000 police officers.

When the NSW Opposition proposed an additional 1,000 police if they were elected to Government, the then Police Commissioner Peter Ryan dismissed the idea and claimed he would be unable to train that number. It successfully destroyed the Opposition's policy for increased numbers of police.

AN AGENDA FOR CHANGE

The NSW Police Force needs reform, but not in the direction it is currently going. I propose the following:

1. Reintroduce the height and weight restrictions we had up until the 1980s. Now more than ever, we need big, tough cops again. We need cops that can't be physically or

mentally intimidated by street gangs.

2. Increase police numbers by 5,000.

3. Re-install some measure of experience into the promotion system, for example promotion to Sergeant at minimum of 10 years service, 15 years for Inspector and 20 years for Superintendent. (This would disallow the example of one police officer who was promoted to Superintendent in 1999 at 33 years of age and placed in charge of a Detective's Unit.)

4. Bring back specialized Detective Squads with proper supervision.

5. Bring back the Summary Offences Act and have a specialized Anti Social Police Squad of at least 500 to operate State-wide.

6. Place emphasis on life experience and attract the tradesman, the family man, ex serviceman into the force.

7. Bring back Police Districts and do away with Regionalisation. It has been a failure and has delivered little other than replicating responsibilities all over the state.

8. Trim down the senior management structure so that Chief Inspectors run large police stations and Inspectors run smaller stations. I have never seen a convincing argument for having hundreds of Superintendents running around NSW on $120,000 annual salary. It was created by Ryan without ever understanding the size of NSW and the different needs of individual police patrols. Having a Superintendent at virtually every station is madness.

9. Bring in part-time police as they do in many other parts of the world. They only need to be used on weekends on special occasions, but having an additional 5,000 to 10,000

trained police to be able to be mobilized quickly is a major insurance policy for the future in these uncertain times.

10. Abolish the right of the Police Minister to dismiss the Commissioner of Police and hand it back either to the Parliament or to the Governor of NSW. The role of Police Commissioner is one of the most important in our society and to have his fate at the hands of one politician, a Minister, begs belief. It is equivalent to handing over the fate of Judges and Magistrates to the Attorney General, so that he can dismiss them if they are performing badly. I guarantee that will never happen.

As *Herald* journalist Miranda Devine once aptly wrote, the NSW Police practised a form of 'reverse broken windows theory', of letting the small crimes develop into bigger ones before the police acted, instead of the proper model of acting on the smaller crimes before they grew into bigger ones.

With the emergence of Middle Eastern and Pacific Islander influenced OMCGs the road ahead for Police in NSW is a rocky one, after years of neglect and inaction. Having outsiders redesign a Police Force has now clearly failed to deliver even the most basic of policing responsibilities—street safety.

What is needed is fresh ideas and a political commitment to fix a police force that just doesn't seem able to get out of second gear. The street cops that do their best day in and day out and are at the mercy of the criminals, their legal counsel, the media and most disturbing of all, their own bosses, need to have the shackles taken off them. They need to be supported by their managers, even when they make mistakes.

An entire society depends on a strong working police force to keep the baddies from getting at the goodies. That's as simple as it gets.

About the Author

At 17, Tim Priest joined the Australian Regular Army where he served for nearly nine years before joining the New South Wales Police Service. After completing his training at the Redfern Police Academy, Tim worked in many of Sydney's toughest crime spots—Redfern, Green Valley, Liverpool, Kings Cross and Cabramatta. A decorated detective, he worked with such criminal investigative units as the National Crime Authority and the Criminal Investigation Branch's drug squad in operations involving organised crime and drug trafficking. Tim was medically retired from the service in August 2002. His first book, *To Protect and To Serve*, a shocking insight into ethnic crime and police bureaucracy, was published in 2003. He served as Chairman of the Prime Minister's Crime Advisory Group (Western Sydney) from 2004-2007. *Enemies of the State* is Priest's second book. He is married to Karen, a registered nurse, and has four children and lives quietly in the outskirts of Sydney.

ACKNOWLEDGMENTS

Special thanks to Mick McGann for his assistance and the use of his article 'Who Guards the Guards'. Also Brian Harding for his help and advice. Thank you to the following for their support: Dr Richard Basham, Frank Reitano, Miranda Devine, Michael Drury, Paul Kenny, Steve Barrett, Glen McNamara, Rob Ovadia, Alan Jones, Charlie Lynn, Malcolm Kerr, Roger Rogerson, Jason Morrison, Ray Hadlee, Peter Kelly, Elyse White, Geoff Featon, Mark Fitzpatrick, Lloyd Martin and Jimmy Harvey.

Special thanks to New Holland Publishing for their faith and encouragement in turning a story into a book, especially Fiona Schultz, Lliane Clarke, Ian Dodd and the many wonderful staff.

My agent Bruce Kennedy for his patience and perserverance.

To the many unnamed cops that helped with putting the puzzle together so that this story could be told.

As always, Ross Treyvaud, for his friendship, loyalty and encouragement.

To Cobbitty General Store, my other 'office'.

Finally to Al Baxter—wherever you are.

REFERENCES

1. FOR THE GOOD OF THE COMMUNITY

1. Drug Misuse and Trafficking Act 1985, Sect 19.

2. Parliament of NSW, Royal Commission into NSW Police Service, Urgent Motion, 11 May 1994.

3. Report(s) of the Royal Commission into the NSW Police (Wood Royal Commission) 1994-1997.

4. Royal Commission into Drug Trafficking (1977–1980) Woodward Royal Commission.

5. 'Who Guards the Guards', An account of illegal actions of the Wood Royal Commission into the NSW Police Service, Detective Michael (Mick) McGann 2003, submission to Legal and Constitutional Affairs, Australian Parliament, 'Bishop' Enquiry.

6. The Commission of Inquiry into Possible Illegal Activities and Associated Police Misconduct (Fitzgerald Inquiry 1989).

7. Report of the Royal Commission into arrest and charging of Harold James Blackburn (Blackburn Royal Commission) (1990).

8. Author interview with former Assistant Police Commissioner Geoff Schuberg.

9. High Court of Australia, *R vs Williams*, 1985.

10. *Sydney Morning Herald*, Kate McClymont, 26 July, 1996.

2. TASK FORCE BAX

1. Report(s) of the Royal Commission into the NSW Police (Wood Royal Commission) 1994-1997.

2. Drug Misuse and Trafficking Act 1985, Sect 19.

3. Australian Parliament, Parliamentary Research Service, Police Entrapment, the High Court decision, *Ridgeway v. the Queen*.

4. Transcript ABC PM Program, 4 September 2008, 'High Court rules NSW Crime Commission drug sting illegal.'

5. Australian Institute of Criminology, *Trends and Issues*, No. 188, Heroin Overdoses and Duty of Care, Paul Williams and Gregor Urbas, February 2001.

6. *Sydney Morning Herald*, 23 July 1996, 'Academic attacks Wood's heroin 'scaremongering'.

7. *Sydney Morning Herald*, 22 July 1996, Heat turned on building owner after Kings Cross drug raids.

8. *Sydney Morning Herald*, 23 July 1996, Chaos and cakes on Menu as Cosmo is hit again.

9. *Sydney Morning Herald*, 26 July 1996, Bill Bayeh's wife charged with drug conspiracy.

10. *Sydney Morning Herald*, 25 July 1996, More witnesses arrested at hearing, *Sydney Morning Herald*, 27 July 1996, Cosmo clan unstuck.

11.NSW Court of Criminal Appeal, Judgment R v Bayeh (2000) NSWCCA 473.

12. Record of surveillance tape conducted between KX15 and Louis Bayeh, 19 July 1996, NSW Police.

13. Wood Royal Commission hearing transcript on 25 July 1996 re Peter Kay (29346) T-291.

14. Wood Royal Commission hearing transcript on 25 July 1996 re Peter Kay (Karamahalis) (29299) T-291.

15. District Court of NSW (Criminal Jurisdiction) Regina v Peter Karamihalis Kay, Bill Bayeh, Michael Dominic Pedavoli. 97/110303 on 17 August 1998, Transcripts of Judgement by DCJ Gibson.

16. District Court of NSW (Criminal Jurisdiction) R v Peter Kay & R v Roula Kay, Judgment on Voir-Dire issues, DCJ Viney QC, 9 December 1999.

17. Wood Royal Commission hearing transcript on 22 July 1996, 'Hot Heroin' incident (29090) T-289.

18. NDARC technical Report No.141, Early Indicators of trends in opoid overdose deaths, Degenhardt, Adelstein, Darke and Hodda, 2002.

19. *Sydney Morning Herald*, The Cocaine, the dealer and the green light, Kate McClymont and Deborah Snow, 6 June, 2008.

20. Complaints to Police Integrity Commission re Task Force Bax, 1999.

21. Report to NSW Police, Executive Director, Human Resources, 1998.

22. Report to PANSW Executive, re Task Force Bax, May 2006.

23. Letter to Irene Moss AO, Independent Commission Against Corruption, 2004.

24. Letter from Irene Moss, Commissioner ICAC, July 2004 to Task Force BAX member.

25. Documents from Task Force Bax re Bayeh, KX15, July 1996.

26. Summary documents presented to Police Integrity Commission re Task Force Bax hearings.

27. Letter of complaint to ICAC re Task Force Bax, 2003.

28. Letter from ICAC re release of ICAC letter to Task Force Bax re investigation of their complaints 2003.

29. Report of PIC investigation into complaint by Task Force Bax members re Wood Royal Commission, dated 16 June 2003.

30. Chronology of events re Task Force Bax.

31. NSW Police Internal Affairs record of interview with Task Force Bax re complaints against WRC and SCIA., 1998.

32. *Sydney Morning Herald* article 25 July 1996, Cosmo snares two more on drug charges.

33. *Sydney Morning Herald* article July 1996, police seize drugs, documents in raid on Bayeh's café.

34. *Sydney Morning Herald*, December 12, 1997, The curious case of the disappearing detective.

35. *Sydney Morning Herald*, 2001, Corrupt Police trapped: how Operation Gymea flowered.

36. *The Daily Telegraph*, December 12, 1997, Shame in the BAX seat.

37. *The Daily Telegraph* – November 26, 1999, Ray Chesterton, The more things change, the more they stay the same.

38. *The Daily Telegraph*, July 26 1996, Bayeh bought off agent.

39. Channel 9, 60 Minutes program, 'Dirty Work' 2003, transcripts from program.

40. *Sydney Morning Herald*, November 29, 1997, 'Double Cross'.

41. *The Australian*, Steve Barrett, Fresh look at Drug Police.

42. Report of the Royal Commission into arrest and charging of Harold James Blackburn (Blackburn Royal Commission) (1990).

43. Official complaint to the Commissioner of Police, NSW Police Force re allegations of impropriety by WRC Investigators Stevens and McGinlay.

44. Record of Surveillance tape conducted between KX15 and Louis Bayeh, 19 July 1996.

45. Author interview with Steve Barrat, July 2008.

46. Report to NSW Parliment by PIC on Operation Jade regarding Task Force Bax, 1998.

3. The Kareela cat burglar

1. Investigation Report of 'Operation Peachface' into allegations of impropriety by members of the Wood Royal Commission.

2. Detective's Statement re arrest and charging of YM1.

3. Email re ICAC investigation of complaints re WRC investigators Stevens and McGinlay.

4. Legal Advice given to DPP re charging of Detectives over arrest and charging of YM1 in 1984.

5. *The Australian*, 3 October 2008, Minister: 'NSW cops most corrupt'.

6. *The Australian*, Steve Barrett, Corruption complaint 'ignored', November, 2003.

7. 'Who Guards the Guards', An account of illegal actions of the Wood Royal Commission into the NSW Police Service, Detective Michael (Mick) McGann 2003, submission to Legal and Constitutional Affairs, Australian Parliament, 'Bishop' Enquiry.

8. Statement by former Detective Glen McNamara re WRC Investigators.

9. Brief of evidence re Court proceedings against Detectives involved in arrest and charging of YM1 in 1984.

10. Transcripts of Judgment of Local Court Magistrate Mr Barnett re YM1 Court matter.

11. *Sydney Morning Herald*, Kate McClymont, Charges against five senior officers, 1 July 1999.

12. Fitzgerald Enquiry reports into Queensland Police Licensing Branch.

13. Wood Royal Commission hearing transcripts re Kareela Cat Burglar Segment – YM1, 24 June, 1996 pp 27430-39.

14. Wood Royal Commission hearing transcripts YM2, 25 June, 1996 pp 27511-26.

15. Wood Royal Commission hearing transcripts YM3, 25 June, 1996 pp 27590-611.

16. Wood Royal Commission hearing transcripts YM4 25-26 June 1996 pp 27635-58 & 27661-86.

17. *Playboy*, Magazine, December 1980 edition, The Toorak Cat.

18. IRC transcript of *Hollingsworth v Commissioner of Police*, NSW IRC 192 (22 December 1997).

4. WHOSE WITNESS? THE BODOR INQUIRY

1. Report by Peter Bodor QC into allegations surrounding the review of allegations made by witness 'James', 2001.
2. NSW Legislative Council Enquiry into Policing in Cabramatta 2000-2002.
3. Transcripts, Exhibits and correspondence from the Bodor Enquiry.
4. Email from Chris Masters ABC Four Corners program to Dr Richard Basham re Jonestown, 4 May, 2002.
5. Parliament of NSW *Hansard* 11 May 2004, James Enquiry Report.
6. NSW Police FOI application re 'James' report.
7. NSW Police 'memo' system, Frank Reitano to Clive Small re Peter Starr.
8. Letter from Michael N Holmes, NSW Police Legal to Cabramatta Enquiry, 23 February, 2001.
9. Letter from Michael N Holmes, NSW Police Legal to Cabramatta Enquiry, 19 April, 2001.
10. Letter from Michael North Holmes, NSW Police Legal to Cabramatta Enquiry, 27 April, 2001.
11. Letter from Michael N Holmes, NSW Police Legal to Cabramatta Enquiry, 1 May, 2001.
12. Letter from Michael North Holmes, NSW Police Legal to Cabramatta Enquiry, 22 June, 2001.
13. Letter from Michael North Holmes, NSW Police Legal to Cabramatta Enquiry, 25 June, 2001.
14. Letter from Michael North Holmes, NSW Police Legal to Cabramatta Enquiry, 18 July, 2002 re Commander Clive Small.
15. Submission to Cabramatta Enquiry by Dr Richard Basham re evidence given by Mike Carlton and Clive Small on 13 August 2002.
16. *Sydney Morning Herald*, Mike Carlton, 'James'.
17. Jonestown, Transcripts of ABC Four Corners program, Chris Masters – May 2002.
18. Bodor Enquiry interviews: Reitano/Basham/Small/Priest/Drury/Wales/Hansen/Wallace/Hiron/James/Appleton/Taylor, 2003/2004.
19. Transcript 60 Minutes, *Gangland*, Ray Martin, Channel 9, 2001.
20. NSW Police COPS event number 16129201, 22 November 1999.

5. OFF THE RECORD

1. Bodor Enquiry Report 2003 into allegations surrounding the review of complaints re witness 'James.'

2. Bodor Enquiry 2003, Transcripts of interviews. Exhibits/ Reports.

3. Legal and Constitutional Affairs, Australian Parliament, 'Bishop' Enquiry, transcripts of proceedings.

4. NSW Police memo system, email from Arnott to Paul Akon, Police Legal Services on 2 December 2003.

6. NSW Police Report compiled by Chief Inspector Bryan Doyle, Police Legal Svcs, 7 February 2005.

7. *Jonestown*, ABC Four Corners, transcripts of program 6 May 2002.

8. Submission to Cabramatta Enquiry by Officers A, B, C & D. Intelligence reports re gangs in schools 2001.

9. Legal Affidavit of 'James' re Appleton/ Small 2003.

10. *The Australian*, Jonestown journalist fires back: 9 May 2007.

11. *Sydney Morning Herald*, The other victims who copped Jones bio hiding. Miranda Devine, 2006.

12. Couriermail.com.au, Fateful trail had dramatic end, Phil Dickie 14 May 2007.

13. Parliament of NSW, *Hansard*, 16 October 2001.

14. Email from Chris Masters to author 26 October 2006 at 9.53pm.

15. Alliance Online, Media Alliance Code of Ethics.

16. Draft Minutes, Internal review Panel Meeting, Police HQ, 3 August 2001.

17. *The Daily Telegraph*, July 31, 2001, Getting the Minister up to scratch.

18. *The Daily Telegraph*, Piers Akerman, Hot potato nobody wants to pick up, 2001.

19. *Sydney Morning Herald*, Linda Doherty, 1 May 2001, Drug dens luring teenagers say Police.

20. *The Daily Telegraph*, Credibility of Police diminished, 13 July, 2001.

21. *The Daily Telegraph*, Police kept documents from judge, Janet Fife-Yeomans: 3 February, 2007.

22. *Sun Herald*, Injection of Police the real life saver, Miranda Devine, 2003.

23. *Sydney Morning Herald*, Four Corners but one-sided, Paul Sheehan: 27 April, 2009.

24. Fax from Grahame Kidd (Principal Cabramatta H.S.) to Hedley Mooney on 19 February 2001 at 3.25pm re 'incident outside the school gates'.

25. Email Author to Chris Masters on 29 October 2006 at 4.05pm re Jonestown

26. Email from Chris Masters to Author 30 October 2006.

27. Email from Author to Chris Masters 14 November 2006 at 22.15pm re Supreme Court Judgement in favour of Alan Jones over Lola Scott.

28. Email from Author to Chris Masters and reply on 9 November 2006 re lola Scott defamation matter.

29. Plaintiffs further submissions on Operation Retz tendered to NSW Supreme Court on 14 November 2006.

30. Confidential submission re Patrol Intelligence Team, Cabramatta 1999.

31. Media release, The Greens: Operation retz report Supreme Court baulks at govt's attempts to hide.

32. Letter from NSW Police Commissioner to Alan Jones on 4 June 2004 re Supt Bruce Newling complaint.

33. Document: Notes re James Complaint, Some issues, authored by Clive Small marked 'E', Bodor Enquiry 2003.

34. Summary of Priest/Basham/Lyons events of 11 April 2002, author/Clive Small, Bodor Enquiry 2003.

35. Letter from Michael N Holmes, Legal Services to Peter Bodor QC re 'Request for Review' on 'James' review: 21 March 2003.

36. *Sunday Telegraph* 19 November 2006, Piers Akerman, State politics in need of a drastic overhaul.

37. *The Daily Telegraph* 21 December 2006, Piers Akerman, Walls tumble down on police secrets.

38. *The Sun Herald*, 2007, Erin O'Dwyer, I never had a problem, but there's a problem now, The interview with Chris Masters ABC.

39. NSW Police, Media release re Commissioner comments on Operation Retz report, 7 December 2006.

40. NSW Parliament, *Hansard* 18 October 2001, Death of Mr Edison Berrio, operation Retz.

41. NSW Parliament, Minutes of Legislative Council on 23 November 2006, Operation Retz.

42. NSW Parliament, *Hansard*, Legislative Council, 19 November 2002, Assistant Commissioner of Police Ms Lola Scott.

43. Parliament of NSW, Legislative Assembly, Q&A 5 May 2004, Operation Retz 1734.

44. Parliament of NSW, *Hansard*, Legislative Council on 23 November 2006.

45. *The Daily Telegraph*, The power of a single vote, Piers Akerman,

25 November 2006.

46. AAP, Old Style alliances threaten the corruption fight, Mark Day: 25 November 2004.

47. *The Sunday Telegraph*, Ethnic youth have NSW Government on the run, Piers Akerman: January 15 2006.

48. *The Australian*, Stop the social engineering and empower Sydney Police, Priest, T, 2005.

49. RMIT University website, Chris Masters, RMIT Honorary award, Chris Masters 2009.

50. *The Australian*, Threats have ABC cowering, Brad Norington: 10 September 2007.

51. EVATT Foundation, A metaphysical lottery, Who Killed investigative journalism, Speech by Chris Masters on 21 February 2003.

52. *The Australian*, Book critics silent about Jones's many scandals, Chris Masters: October 28, 2006.

53. *The Australian*, Search for the truth liberates ABC veteran Chris Masters, November 17 2008.

54. 'Truth, politics and the limits of investigative journalism', Alan Knight, Central Queensland University: 2 May 2002.

55. *Sins of the Brothers*, Mark Whittaker and Les Kennedy: Pan MacMillan 2002.

56. NSW Legislative Assembly, *Hansard*, 16 November 1994, Mr. Keith Waite sexual assault allegations.

57. *The Electronic Whorehouse*, Paul Sheehan: Pan MacMillan 2003.

58. Meeting between Chris Masters and Author at Central R.S. on 1 May 2005.

59. Interview with former Detective Inspector Michael Drury: March 2009.

60. Interview with Former Detective Sergeant Roger Caleb Rogerson: February 2009.

61. Interview with former Assistant Commissioner of Police (Internal Affairs), NSW Police, Geoff Schuberg.

62. Interview with Sergeant Frank Reitano, NSW Police, February, 2009.

63. Video Chris Masters at Mosman Library, Jonestown: November 15, 2006.

64. *R v Ivan Milat* NSWSC 1996.

65. CIA (Crime Investigation Australia) Foxtel, The backpacker murders.

66. ABC *7.30 Report* with Kerry O'Brien, Interview with Chris Masters: Jonestown.

67. *Sydney Morning Herald*, Books: review by Chris Masters on Peter Ryan, *The Inside Story*: Sue Williams: Viking 2002.

68. *The Australian*, October 30 2006, Professor David Flint.

69. *Sydney Morning Herald*, Mike Carlton, 3 April 2004, What to tell Mr Howard.

6. UNDER THE RADAR: THE WINCHESTER CASE

1. Australian Federal Police website, Murder of Assistant Commissioner Winchester, January 10, 1989.

2. ParlInfo, Page One, Channel 10, A Capital Offence, Chris Masters, 24 April, 1989, Program transcripts.

3. ParlInfo, Page One, Channel 10, A Capital Offence, Chris Masters, 1 May, 1989, Program transcripts.

4. *Enough Rope*, Andrew Denton/interview with Chris Masters 3 November 2008

5. *The Australian*, David Flint: 30 October, 2006.

6. ParlInfo, *Hansard*, Senate, 24 May, 1989.

7. High Court of Australia, *David Harold Eastman v DPP ACT*, 28 May 2003.

8. Media Release by John Stanhope, ACT Chief Minister re conviction of David Eastman for the murder of Assistant Commissioner Colin Winchester, 10 October 2005.

9. *Canberra Times*, 10 October 2004, Winchester Murder trial, fair or not?

10. *Sydney Morning Herald*, 16 December, 2003, Canberra decides transporting its prisoners is a capital offence.

11. *R v David Harold Eastman* (1995) ACTSC 59, Murder.

12. *Eastman v The Attorney-general for the ACT* (2007) ACTSC 28.

13. *Eastman v The Hon Jeffrey Miles & Ors* (2004) ACTSC 32.

14. *Eastman v The Honourable Chief Justice Terrence John Higgins* (2007).

15. *Eastman v The Hon Jeffery Alan Miles* (2006) ACTSC 49.

16. *Eastman v The Hon Jeffrey Alan Miles* (2006) ACTSC 57.

17. *Eastman v The Hon Jeffrey Allan Miles* (2006) ACTSC 27.

18. *Eastman v the Honourable Justice Besanko* (2009) ACTSC 10.

19. Australian Capital Territory Consolidated Acts, Crimes Act 1900, Sect 396, Public Mischief.

20. Legislative Assembly for the Australian Capital Territory, *Hansard* 19 October, 1995.

21. Police Integrity Commission media release re Operation Florida hearings, 2001.

22. Report by the Inspector of the Police Integrity Commission re Four Corners program: 8 October 2001, Preliminary Investigation.

23. *Hansard*, NSW Parliament, 16 October 2001, Operation Florida.

24. *Hansard*, NSW Parliament—16 October 2001, Operation Florida/Police Minister.

25. *Hansard*, NSW Parliament, 18 October 2001, Four Corners program.

26. PIC Hearing details, Operation Florida, 10 August 2001.

27. Transcript from PM Program, ABC Radio, 8 October 2001, NSW Police Corruption Inquiry.

28. *Sydney Morning Herald*, 29 June 2004, Police clean-out but rot goes on.

29. Parliament of NSW, Committee on the Office of the Ombudsman and the Police Integrity Commission, Phase two of an inquiry into Section 10 (5) of the PIC Act 1996, Transcripts of proceedings.

30. Report by Police Integrity Commission into circumstances surrounding the Four Corners program on 8 October 2001.

31. Parliament of NSW, Report of 5th General meeting with Inspector of the PIC, 16 October 2003.

32. NSW Consolidated Acts, Police Integrity Commission Act 1996, Sect 118: 'Contempt'.

33. NSW Consolidated Acts, Police Integrity Commission Act 1996, Sect 121: Act or omission that is both an offence and contempt.

34. Report of the Royal Commission into the NSW Police (Wood Royal Commission) 1994-1997, definition of corruption/noble cause/process corruption.

35. *Not for publication*, Chris Masters, ABC Books.

7. True Crime?

1. *The Age* 27 May 2002, 'Police yet to discover what sparked Cabramatta shooting'.

2. *Sydney Morning Herald*, Mike Carlton, 31 May 2002, 'Lunching on the mean streets of Cabramatta'.

3. *The Daily Telegraph*, April 23, 2009, 'Carlton below belt'.

4. *The Daily Telegraph*, Fiona Connolly, July 19 2007, 'Zemanek slur puts Carlton's career on the line'.

5. *Sydney Morning Herald*, 28 May 2006, Mike Carlton, Coverage of the Cronulla Riots.

6. *Sydney Morning Herald*, March 29, 2009, Les Kennedy, 'The rise and rise of new gangs'.

7. *Sydney Morning Herald*, 10 July 2002, Miranda Devine, 'Cabramatta then, now and post-poll.

8. *The Daily Telegraph*, 2 February 2007, Rhett Watson, 'Clive Small quits ICAC'.

9. *Sydney Morning Herald*, 18 May 2007, Mike Carlton, 'Let me tell you about the copper deal'.

10. *Sydney Morning Herald*, 16 August 2002, Mike Carlton, 'Threats against Carlton'.

11. *Sydney Morning Herald* 28 May 2006, Mike Carlton ' The case for the damnation of Marsden'.

12. *Sydney Morning Herald*, October 28-29 2006, Mike Carlton, 'Jonestown'.

13. *The Daily Telegraph*, 18 July 2007, Fiona Connolly, 'I loathed Zemanek, says Carlton.'

14. Correspondence from 2UE, R.G. (Bob) Miller, General Manager, dated April 5 2005.

15. Transcripts 2UE program 3.08pm 12 July 2001, Mike Carlton on Cabramatta Policing.

16. Transcripts 2UE program 4.08 pm on 12 July 2001, Mike Carlton, Interview with opposition police spokesman Andrew Tink.

17. Transcripts of 2UE program 5.16pm 6 February 2002, Mike Carlton and Police Minister Michael Costa.

18. Transcripts 2UE program 4.13pm, 28 May 2002, Mike Carlton and Police Minister Michael Costa.

19. Transcripts 2UE program 8.09am, 20 May 2004, Mike Carlton talking about Redfern Riots.

20. Inthemix Forums.com.au, Mike Carlton comments on Alan Jones on release of 'Jonestown'.

21. *City Journal*, Autumn 2003, Theodore Dalrymple, 'Barbarians at the gates of Paris'.

22. Speech, Priest, T: The Rise of Middle Eastern Crime in Australia, *Quadrant magazine*, 2003.

23. Report by Peter Bodor QC into allegations surrounding the review of allegations made by witness 'James', 2001.

8. SYDNEY CONFIDENTIAL

1. Submission by Commander C.Small to GPSC No. 3 (Cabramatta Policing) 27 February 2001.

2. NSW Parliament, GPSC No. 3 (Cabramatta Policing) Transcripts, 27 February 2001.

3. *Sydney Morning Herald*, Neil Mercer, 13 February 2003, PIC, Operation Malta Report.

4. *Sydney Morning Herald*, Neil Mercer & Stephen Gibbs, 4 May 2002, 'Man who nailed Milat aims for Ryan's job.'

5. *Sydney Morning Herald*, 9 February 2002, Neil Mercer, 'Rank of Survivor'.

6. *Sydney Morning Herald*, 10 June 2001, Alex Mitchell, 'Testing times for the force.' 8.e SMH, 17 June 2001, Alex Mitchell, 'Drugs capital thrived as Police turned a 'blind eye.'

7. *Sydney Morning Herald*, 31 December 2000, Candace Sutton & Alex Mitchell, 'Police reformer was Lib activist.'

8. *Sydney Morning Herald*, 2 February 1997, Alex Mitchell, 'From the ashes of the CIB, a Detective Force is Resurrected.'

9. Police Integrity Commission 2003, Operation Malta Report, 7.53, 7.54, 7.55, 7.56, 7.57.

10. Bodor Report 8 August 2003, Transcripts of interview, Sgt Frank Reitano.

11. *The Daily Telegraph* 1 May 2001, David Penberthy, 'Students act as drug couriers.'

12. ABC Four Corners, *Jonestown*, 2002, Transcripts from program.

13. *The Australian*, 8 April 2009, Fairfax to pay $1m for Obeid Defamation.

14. 5th National Investigations Symposium, 4-5 November 2004.

15. ABC *Lateline*, 16 March 2003, Transcripts, 'Crime Boss' slaying could lead to gang war.

16. ABC *Stateline*, 8 February 2002, Transcripts of program.

17. Submission to the Parliamentary Privileges and Ethics Committee, October 2001.

18. *Sydney Morning Herald*, July 30 2001, Darren Goodsir, 'Blue Murder justice: how the good cop finished last.'

20. FOI application NSW Police, Documents created by Crime Agencies regarding transfer.

21. NSW Police Memo System 14 May 2001, Commander Small to LAC Commanders Greater Hume.

22. Report from PIC Liaison Unit SCIA, NSW Police 19 July 2002

23. *The Daily Telegraph*, 2 November 2006, Fairfax reporter assault case adjourned

24. News.com.au/story, 'Crime Reporter on gun charge.

25. *The Australian*, Amanda Meade, 17 August 2006, 'Assault on accuracy.'

26. *Sydney Morning Herald* 24 July 2007, Jennifer Cooke, 'Alan Jones pays up for defamation.'

27. *The Sunday Telegraph*, Neil Mercer, 18 March 2007, Shock jocks legal battles.'

28. *The Australian*, 'Trials of the best man.'

29. *Sydney Morning Herald*, 25 January 2004, Candace Sutton, 'Secret reports into gangs go missing.'

30. *The Sunday Telegraph*, 1 February 2004, Neil Mercer, Revealed, report Police wanted to hide.'

32. *Sunday Tasmanian*, 17 July 2005 Marnie O'Neill, Neil Mercer, Leah Creighton, 'Helper known' to Milat Family.

33. *Sydney Morning Herald*, 14 August 2002, Mark Riley, Conspiracy, threats, trumpet blowing: another day at police enquiry.'

34. *Sydney Morning Herald*, 22 May 2004, Mike Carlton 'Politicking over Redfern.'

35. Fairfax Digital, 14 May 2005, 'Slipping the net: the life and crimes of Mr Big'.

36. Letter from John Marsden to Author on 10 March 2004 re Clive Small.

37. ICAC media release 29 April 2004, 'ICAC Commissioner responds to questions raised by Peter Debnam.'

38. Media release by Peter Debnam MP, Shadow Minister for Police, 'Questions for the Commissioner of the ICAC.'

39. *The Daily Telegraph*, July 27 2001, David Penberthy, 'The secret evidence of life in Cabramatta.'

40. *Sydney Morning Herald*, 2001, Marian Wilkinson & Mathew Moore, Police tall poppy lashes out over malicious dirt file.

41. *Sydney Morning Herald*, October 7-8 2006, Emily Dunn, 'Vibrant community beats its gang rap.'

42. *Sunday Herald* 8 October 2006, Llouise Hall and AAP, Court told of $93m laundering operation.'

43. *Sydney Morning Herald*, Stephen Gibbs, 3 September 2003, 'Top detective loses job, but doesn't know why.'

44. *Sydney Morning Herald*, Stephen Gibbs, 14 November 2001, 'Drugs Capital loses its crown.'

45. 3. Report(s) of the Royal Commission into the NSW Police (Wood Royal Commission) 1994-1997.

46. Channel 9, 60 Minutes program, *Dirty Work*, 2003, transcripts from program.

9. The stark reality of policing in NSW

1. Speech, Priest, T, The Rise of Middle Eastern Crime in Australia, *Quadrant magazine*, 2003.

2. Green Left weekly news, 4 February 2004.

3. Gangs of Oz, Channel 7, 2009.

4. *Sunday Telegraph*, 7 June 2009, 'Get serious about gang warfare.'

5. *To Protect and to Serve*, New Holland Publishers, 2003.

6. *The Daily Telegraph*, 6 May 2009, Janet Fife-Yeomans and Kara Lawrence, 'Middle Eastern Youth.'

7. www.wapolun.org.au/getfile.pdf

8. *Sydney Morning Herald*, Miranda Devine.

READ THE EXPLOSIVE BOOK
TO PROTECT AND TO SERVE

Only available as an ebook

www.newholland.com.au/toprotectandtoserve